TIMES CHANGE

The Minimum Wage and
The New York Times

TIMES CHANGE

The Minimum Wage and
The New York Times

Richard B. McKenzie

Pacific Research Institute for Public Policy
San Francisco, California

ISBN 0-936488-76-X

Printed in the United States of America
10   9   8   7   6   5   4   3   2   1

PACIFIC RESEARCH INSTITUTE FOR PUBLIC POLICY
755 Sansome Street, Suite 450
San Francisco, CA 94111
(415) 989-0833

Distributed to the trade by National Book Network, Lanham, MD.

Library of Congress Cataloging-in-Publication Data
McKenzie, Richard B.
    Times change : the minimum wage and the New York times / by Richard B. McKenzie.
        p.   cm.
    Includes index.
    ISBN 0-936488-76-X
    1. Minimum wage in the press—United States. 2. New York times.
I. Title.
PN4899.N42M35   1994
070.4′493312′3—dc20   94-15800
                                                                     CIP

Director of Publications: *Kay Mikel*
Cover Design: *Arrowgraphics Inc.*
Interior Graphics: *Reider Publishing Services*
Index: *Shirley Kessel, Primary Sources Research*
Printing and Binding: *Data Reproductions Corporation*

DEDICATION

for Frank O'Connell

FOREWORD

Newspapers provide facts for our consideration—facts that allow us to make informed judgments of our own about important public policy issues. The editorial page provides a stark contrast to this fact-finding function. Editorials waggle a finger at us, urging some opinion or course of action that goes beyond the facts of the matter at hand.

Yet readers are likely to find editorials somewhat mysterious. No one signs them. Seemingly, no one takes responsibility for them. If the newspaper bothers to offer an explanation, it generally falls in the category of "editorials are expressions of the opinions of the newspaper's management." In the case of small town newspapers with limited staff, the explanation may be literally accurate—the editor of the newspaper, in collaboration with its publisher, or the publisher, with the co-operation of the editor (they may indeed be the same person), writes the editorials. In a big city newspaper, the editor of the news columns is too busy to write editorials. The publisher, who is primarily concerned with managing the newspaper, has no time to write editorials either. That, however, does not mean that the management of the newspaper, as personified by its publisher, plays no part in the process of editorializing. Individual newspapers have individual characters, established over the years by a set of attitudes, a world view, and a generalized political orientation.

In *Times Change*, Richard McKenzie opens the editorial pages of the *New York Times* for our review with regard to minimum wage legislation. McKenzie points out that over several score of years the *Times* editors have talked out of both sides of their mouths, as it were, in presenting the case for or against minimum wage legislation. This chronicle of events is worth a hard look, and McKenzie is thorough and accurate in his portrayal of the editorials published in the *Times*.

But a newspaper editorial page is more than a set of facts, indeed, it is intended to go beyond the facts. As an opinion leader, the *New York Times* has an opportunity to influence both people and policy. So, let's take a look at what drives the editorial page opinions at the *Times*.

In political and economic matters, the *Times* believes in two imperatives. The first is the necessity to adopt such government programs as will help assure the efficient functioning of the private economic system, the only way in which a satisfactory standard of living can be produced for the people of the United States. The second imperative, which must somehow work in tandem with the first, is that even at some risk of interference in the efficiency of the private economy steps must be taken to assure that an adequate share of goods and services be available to every American. Defining, at specific moments in history, exactly what is meant by "adequate," "available," and "the extent to which interference with productive efficiency" will be tolerated is a task for those responsible for composing the *Times* editorials dealing with economic policy.

To judge whether specific government or private economic acts or speeches by public officials or other prominent citizens fairly balance the two imperatives, the *New York Times* relies on ten or eleven full-time members of the editorial board and their leader, the editor of the editorial page. The publisher appoints the members of the editorial board, usually on the recommendation of the editor of the editorial page. The members of the board have no formal connection with the members of the news staff of the *Times*. The overwhelming majority of members of the editorial board are either journalists who developed a specialty interest in the course of their careers or former academics. The editorial board tends to lack members with practical experience within the field about which they write. Those who write about foreign affairs have been foreign correspondents or staff members of institutions dedicated to the exploration of foreign affairs rather than former members of the Foreign Service. Editorial writers on local politics have rarely been politicians. Writers on economics have rarely been business proprietors or labor union officials.

Picking the editor of the editorial page is also a function of the publisher, and exercising that right of choice is a very careful operation. The publisher wants someone with all the professional skills of editorship but, as much, wants a person imbued with the culture of the *Times,* the tone that it seeks to achieve on the page, its fundamental assumptions as to national policy, and its vision of its readership, particularly that part of its readership that more or less regularly consults the editorial page and from time to time expresses opinions in letters to the paper.

Changes in the editorship do occur, as do changes of publishers. There have been four publishers of the *New York Times* since legislation establishing a minimum wage was first introduced. That the *Times* should have taken different positions on the basic issues involved in a minimum wage is not surprising given the two imperatives it seeks to balance: economic efficiency and individual protection against excessive hardship.

I have no way of knowing how the editorial board in December 1937 came to its decisions on questions of the day when the board first expressed an opinion on the proposal for a federal minimum wage. But if matters went as they did during my years on the board, the editor asked the board member who specialized in economics for his view of the minimum wage. That opened the discussion in which members joined, whatever their specialty. The editor closed the discussion and made the final decision. If that decision differed from what the specialist on the issue expressed at the start of the discussion, the specialist might plead that he could not conscientiously write an editorial expressing the opinion the editor wanted expressed. The editors with whom I worked accepted that and either found some other member of the board who would write the editorial or, more frequently, wrote it themselves.

Since the editorial that appeared on December 9, 1937, opposed the minimum wage, I can assume with little risk that the economics writer was also opposed to it. It is quite possible that every economics writer who ever served on the editorial board of the *New York Times* was opposed to the minimum wage, though I have no way of knowing whether or not that was the case. In 1937, the national economy was in a sudden recession from the mild recovery of the previous year. A minimum wage proposal would do nothing to increase the efficiency of the economy; it would merely tend to benefit some persons employed at low wages while caus-ing some other persons employed at low wages to lose their jobs—jobs not worth as much as the minimum wage would cost the employer. The counter-argument, that people employed at low wages are entitled to be protected against undue hardship by higher wages, would make little sense in this environment. In a recession, when manufacturers are having trouble disposing of goods at their current price levels, anything that might increase their costs would tend to reduce their sales, leading to lay-offs and stagnation.

It is easy enough to imagine that in the postwar inflation—as the wage level of unionized workers was rising with some rapidity and prices were rising as well—the discussion on the editorial board would have emphasized the second of the two imperatives, protecting the weak. The economy was operating at prodigious efficiency. The demand for goods was such that prices were rising. Under this set of facts, those members of the editorial board not primarily interested in economics would probably be concerned that workers lacking union membership and working at very low wages were altogether lacking protection against the deprivation resulting from higher prices for consumer goods while their incomes were stagnating. They might have argued that with the economy running close to capacity and unemployment figures very low, an increase in the mini-mum wage would not cause many low-skilled workers to lose their jobs because few unemployed workers at higher skills would be available to take their places. Since the first imperative was, so to speak, taking care of itself, the board might well conclude, with the sensibility of non-economists, that the second imperative—the need to protect the weak—deserved precedence.

At a later stage in the postwar economy, the annual rate of inflation reached new highs and, simultaneously and curiously, the rate of unemployment rose and the economy went into a period of stagnation. Now the first imperative became supremely important. Driven by forces that pushed wages and prices up, inflationary fears that drove interest rates, and new regulatory standards, the economy lost a significant part of its productivity and efficiency. The passage of any law that would increase the upward pressure on wages seemed a further threat to personal security. Those who had supported minimum wage laws because they offered protection to some of the weakest elements in the society were silenced by the havoc they saw around them. It should not surprise anyone that the *Times* shifted again and opposed a raise in the minimum wage. You do not have to be an economist to understand that a major function of minimum wage laws is to make it easier for the unionized worker to receive still higher wages in order to emphasize the gap between his skills (and organization) and the skills of the non-unionized worker. Instead of narrowing the gap, the minimum wage laws expanded it.

The *New York Times*, for better or worse, is not a teacher of economics, although it has had distinguished economists writing for it for many years. It is, in a sense, both more and less than an economics teacher; it is trying to draw the outlines of a good society, which it assumes with some reason cannot be achieved by economics alone. Sometimes, in that effort to achieve a humane balance, the *Times* editors advocate steps that, in retrospect, have made the imbalance greater, not less. It is, after all, a newspaper, probably the best we have, perhaps the best anyone can have. For that reason, many of its admirers feel a pang of regret when, in following its own pole star, it takes a turn in what some are clever enough to know is in the wrong direction.

Richard McKenzie's book explains in relatively simple and clear language what minimum wage legislation does and does not accomplish. McKenzie is an economist, and he is a teacher. What he has to teach us in these pages is that the noble goal of caring for the truly needy cannot be accomplished if we fly in the face of economic facts. While the *Times* editors have tried to strike a balance between two imperatives, McKenzie shows us that the actual results of this balancing act do not help the poor.

Roger Starr
May 16, 1994

CONTENTS

PART II

The Economics of the Minimum Wage   73

PREFACE

President Bill Clinton and Secretary of Labor Robert Reich call themselves "New Democrats." However, in their search for ways to help low-income workers, they have returned to support of an old policy—a hike in the minimum wage—favored by Democrats since at least the late 1930s. They have proposed raising the minimum wage to $4.75 or more (with the actual hike contingent on what happens to their proposed reforms of the health care system).

As shown in this book, President Clinton and Secretary Reich's policy position stands in sharp contrast to the editorial stance of the *New York Times*, widely presumed to be the defender of liberalism. The editors of the *Times* recommend nothing more than a truly *minimum* minimum wage, *zero*. Their reasoning is simple: The minimum wage destroys low wage jobs, precisely the opposite of what government should be doing. As will become evident in the following pages, however, the editors have not always been ardent opponents to the minimum wage. Indeed, they have in the past supported minimum-wage increases with the same vigor and rhetorical flourish that they now oppose them. The fact that the editors have changed their stance on this policy issue should not be surprising, but the importance of the most recent shift to opposition, and the editors' reasoning for their current stance, should not be overlooked by minimum-wage supporters. As the *Times* editors recommend, Congress and the administration should not undercut the economic well-being of low wage workers in their misguided efforts to help them.

ACKNOWLEDGMENTS

I am indebted to a number of people who helped with this project. Clark Nardinelli read the manuscript and made many critical comments and suggestions for improvement. Keith Atkinson, Lynda Lee, Jinju Qian, and Edwina Wicker provided helpful research assistance. Greta Brooks and Karen McKenzie made many editorial improvements. Robert Racine expertly edited the final draft.

I am grateful to several foundations for support during the time this book was completed. The Earhart Foundation provided a grant under which much of the initial research and writing was done. The final draft was completed under grants provided by the John M. Olin Foundation and the Lynde and Harry Bradley Foundation.

"The idea of using a minimum wage to overcome poverty is old, honorable—and fundamentally flawed. It's time to put this hoary debate behind us, and find a better way to improve the lives of people who work very hard for very little."

The editors of the *New York Times*
January 14, 1987

PART I

THE *NEW YORK TIMES* CHANGING EDITORIAL POSITION

CHAPTER 1

The Rocky History

The Clinton administration served notice early in 1993 that it intended to seek an increase in the federal minimum wage.[1] Liberals applauded the new president, agreeing that an increase was deserved. Conservatives lamented the policy proposal, fearful that another minimum-wage increase would further unsettle the economic recovery that was under way at the time. Both liberals and conservatives began to marshal their statistical forces to support long-held claims concerning the positive and negative consequences of another minimum-wage increase.

Contrary to what might be presumed, the most articulate, effective, and ardent opponents of the minimum wage are neither former officials in the Reagan administration, nor the economists who write for professional journals like the *Wall Street Journal* and the *National Review*, but the editors at the *New York Times*. These premier critics don't merely oppose increasing the minimum wage—they advocate its abolition. The editors' current hostility to the minimum wage stands in sharp contrast to their image as defenders of East Coast liberalism, but that contrast makes their opposition noteworthy. What makes the editors current policy all the more striking is that it emerged from a sincere effort in the 1960s and 1970s to maintain their support for just about every proposed increase in the federal minimum wage.

The "Right Minimum Wage"

Early in 1987, the editors of the *New York Times* took a stance that must have shocked many of their occasional readers, liberal and conservative alike: They threw their considerable prestige and political weight against the Democrats' three-step plan for a 39 percent increase in the minimum wage by 1990. Indeed, the editors announced their opposition with a memorably stark headline in a lead editorial: "The Right Minimum Wage: $0.00."[2] That single headline probably did more than any other political

3

commentary of the year to add credibility to the Reagan administration's staunch opposition to any minimum-wage increase and to ensure that an increase would be postponed for (as it turned out to be) two years.[3] Officials in the Reagan administration, openly hostile to most forms of government interventions in labor markets, and the editors at the *Times*, the widely supposed bastion of East Coast liberalism, made for strange bedfellows in that both obviously wanted to abolish altogether the minimum. Their only difference was that the editors openly proposed abolition while Reagan officials only openly opposed additional increases.

The *Times* editors argued that because the minimum wage reduces the employment opportunities of many disadvantaged workers, the federal minimum-wage floor should be eliminated altogether. They acknowledged that the concept of alleviating poverty via minimum-wage increases had an old and honorable tradition, but one that was "fundamentally flawed." They concluded, "It's time to put this hoary debate behind us, and find a better way to improve the lives of people who work very hard for very little." The editors supported hourly wage subsidies based on a test of family means (or income) (Jan. 14, 1987).

While this seemingly new editorial position may have shocked occasional readers, faithful and careful readers could see that the papers' stark editorial position on the issue had been seesawing from a position of adamant opposition when the federal minimum wage was first proposed and passed in the late 1930s, to equally adamant support, then back to complete opposition for the previous decade. This book charts the gradual (and somewhat reluctant) shift in the *New York Times* position as articulated in at least 121 major editorials printed over the fifty-seven years from 1937 (the year in which the first federal minimum wage that became law was proposed) to 1993,[4] the book focuses on the reasoning for these vastly different positions.

This review of the *Times* editorials provides a clear example of how the ideas and empirical work by a host of applied microeconomists influenced the policy position adopted by "the most influential paper not just in the country but the world."[5] The review also shows how, before the 1970s, a changing group of editorial writers presented some highly sophisticated and technical arguments against adoption of the first federal minimum-wage law, a position and manner of presentation eventually abandoned in favor of highly charged emotional appeals for increases in the federal minimum wage as a matter of "simple justice." Years later, however, in light of a growing body of evidence, the editors began to seek a "sensible compromise" on minimum-wage increases (one that would destroy some, but not too many, jobs). And then finally, in light of "virtual unanimous" opposition among economists to the minimum wage, they called for defeat of a proposed increase, a position that later was converted into a call for the complete abolition of the minimum—state or federal.[6] The gradual shift in the position of prominent national opinion makers, such as the *New York Times* editors, may go a long way toward explaining the rise and fall of the real-dollar purchasing power of the minimum wage over the course of its history.

The Nominal and Real Minimum Wage

The first U.S. federal minimum wage was incorporated into the Fair Labor Standards Act and was set in nominal-dollar terms at 25 cents an hour for 1938.[7] As of 1989, the nominal minimum wage had been adjusted upward through the passage of seven amendments to the Fair Labor Standards Act, which, because several of the amendments scheduled a series of annual adjustments, have resulted in eighteen changes in the nominal dollar value of the federal minimum wage.[10] As reported in Table 1.1, the nominal minimum wage rose to 30 cents in 1939 and to 40 cents in 1945. It did not reach $1 until 1956 and $2 until 1974. The minimum wage remained at $3.35 an hour between 1981 and 1990. In November 1989, Congress passed, and President Bush signed, legislation to raise the minimum wage to $3.80 in April 1990 and then to $4.25 a year later, when they added, for the first time, a subminimum training wage for teenagers at 85 percent of the adult minimum ($3.61 an hour in 1991).[9]

The changing fortunes of minimum-wage workers relative to other hourly workers can be attributed mainly to changes in the real purchasing power of the minimum wage. As Figure 1.1 shows, the nominal-dollar minimum wage has ratcheted upward, but the real-dollar minimum wage has varied considerably over the years. The minimum rose gradually but irregularly in real-dollar terms (February 1993 prices) from $2.54 an hour in 1938 to $6.58 in 1968—an increase of 159 percent in purchasing power. After 1968, however, the real value of the minimum began a gradual but bumpy slide until, in 1993, its real (and legislated nominal) value stood at $4.25, 5 percent less than the real minimum in 1950 and 24 percent less than the minimum in 1968. Assuming Congress does not raise the nominal minimum again and assuming an annual inflation rate of 4 percent between 1993 and 1996, the real purchasing power in 1996 of the adult minimum wage will be $3.78 an hour, slightly more (3 cents) per hour than the real value of the minimum in 1989, 13 percent less than the real minimum in 1950, and 42 percent less than the minimum in 1968.

TABLE 1.1 Legislative history of the federal minimum wage

Legislation	Date passed	Minimum wage	Effective date
Fair Labor Standards Act of 1938	June 25, 1938	$ .25	October 24, 1938
		$ .30	October 24, 1939
		$ .40	October 24, 1945
1949 Amendment	October 26, 1949	$ .75	January 24, 1950
1955 Amendment	August 12, 1955	$1.00	March 1, 1956
1961 Amendment	May 5, 1961	$1.15	September 3, 1961
		$1.25	September 3, 1963
1966 Amendment	September 23, 1966	$1.40	February 1, 1967
		$1.60	February 1, 1968
1974 Amendment	April 2, 1974	$2.00	May 1, 1974
		$2.10	January 1, 1975
		$2.30	January 1, 1976
1977 Amendment	November 1, 1977	$2.65	January 1, 1978
		$2.90	January 1, 1979
		$3.10	January 1, 1980
		$3.35	January 1, 1981
		Adult minimum	
1989 Amendment	November 9, 1989	$3.80	April 3, 1990
		$4.25	April 3, 1991
		Teenage minimum	
		$3.23	April 3, 1990
		$3.61	April 3, 1991

Source: U.S. Department of Health and Human Services, Social Security Administration, *Social Security Bulletin: Annual Statistical Supplement, 1990* (Washington, DC: U.S. Government Printing Office, December 1990), p. 105.

FIGURE 1.1 The minimum wage in current and constant
(February 1993) dollars, 1938–1993

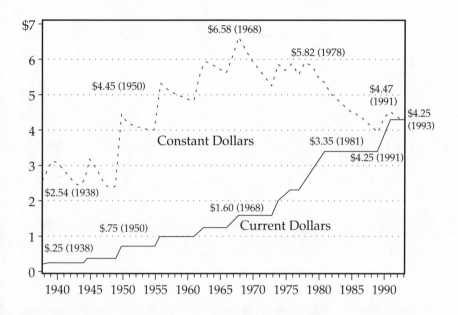

Source: *Social Security Bulletin, Annual Statistical Supplement, 1992,* and author's
calculations.

The minimum wage also began to fall relative to the hourly wage of
higher paid workers at about the same time as did its real purchasing
power. When the minimum was first instituted in 1938, it was slightly
above 40 percent of the average hourly earnings of manufacturing production workers. As Figure 1.2 shows, the minimum rose to 58 percent of
the average wage of nonsupervisory and nonagricultural workers in 1950
and stayed close to or above 50 percent of that wage base for most of the
1950s and 1960s. After jumping temporarily back to 57 percent of the
average hourly earnings in 1968, the minimum wage fell precipitously
until in 1989 it equaled only 35 percent of average hourly earnings, only
to jump back up to 41 percent in 1991 and then fall slightly to 40 percent
in 1992.

Often, the falloffs in both the real and relative values of the minimum
wage have been blamed on politics, mainly the ascendancy of Ronald
Reagan to the presidency. Note, however, that more than half ($1.31) of
the erosion in the minimum real value since 1968 ($2.33) occurred before

7

FIGURE 1.2 The minimum wage as a percentage of the average wage of nonagricultural workers, 1947–1992

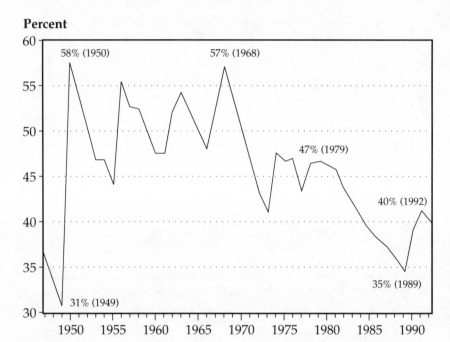

Source: *Economic Report of the President,* various years, *Social Security Bulletin, Annual Statistical Supplement, 1992,* and author's calculations.

1981, the year Reagan took office. That fact, along with the observation that both houses of Congress were controlled by the Democrats for most of the years between 1968 and 1989, suggests that the decline in the real value of the minimum wage cannot be attributed solely to the ideological obstinacy of the Reagan administration. Granted, Reagan and most of his key advisors staunchly opposed any upward adjustment of the nominal minimum, but significant political support for their position must have come from Democrats who no longer saw the minimum as an effective means of helping low-wage workers.

The percentage of the American labor force covered by the federal minimum wage also expanded over the decades, which may be just as important in determining the political (and media) acceptability of mini-mum-wage adjustments as the adjustments themselves. Figure 1.3 shows that the number of workers covered by the minimum grew substantially

FIGURE 1.3 Minimum wage coverage rate for nonagricultural employment, 1950–1988

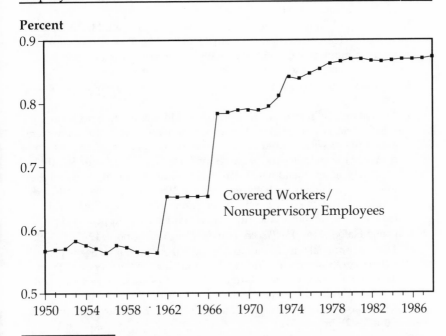

Percent

Source: Marvin H. Kosters, *Jobs and the Minimum Wage, The Effect of Changes in the Level and Pattern* (Washington, DC: American Enterprise Institute, 1989), p. A-13.

over the years. The original minimum-wage law applied mainly to workers directly involved in interstate commerce. However, as court decisions gradually expanded the definition of interstate commerce and as more groups of workers were explicitly included, the labor force covered rose to 57 percent of total nonagriculture (nonsupervisory) employment in 1950, 65 percent in 1962, 79 percent in 1967, 84 percent in 1974, and finally, to an estimated 87 percent in 1980, where it remained, more or less, through 1988 (the last year of available data).[10]

As will be seen, the *Times* editorials on the minimum wage are a historical account of the ideas for and against government aid to low-wage workers. This record has value because of the importance of the *New York Times* as a political force and because the *Times* dramatically shifted its editorial position on the minimum wage on several occasions, defending each new stance with no less vigor than it exerted for its previous position.

Notes

1. Steven Greenhouse, "Clinton Delays Push to Increase Minimum Wage," *New York Times*, June 6, 1993, p. A1.

2. "The Right Minimum Wage: $0.00," *New York Times*, Jan. 14, 1987, editorial, p. 18. Henceforth, references to the major *New York Times* editorials on the minimum wage will be by editorial dates in parentheses in text. Full references to these editorials appear in Appendix A.

3. Congress did not pass an increase in the minimum wage until November 1989.

4. The listing of editorials in Appendix A includes only those pieces in which *Times* editors made substantive comments on the minimum-wage and hours provisions (and to hours provisions when parallels were drawn between hours and wage restrictions) of the Fair Labor Standards Act and its amendments. A number of editorials that discussed the minimum wage written between 1937 and 1989 have not been included because they made only passing reference to minimum-wage laws. Fifteen of the more important editorials are reprinted in Appendix B.

5. David Halberstam, *The Powers That Be* (New York: Knopf, 1979), p. 219.

6. The conventional way economists analyze the minimum wage is provided in graphic form in Chapter 7. For a review of the economic literature on the minimum wage through the early 1980s, see Charles Brown, Curtis Gilroy, and Andrew Cohen, "The Effect of the Minimum Wage on Employment and Unemployment," *Journal of Economic Literature* (June 1982), pp. 487–528.

7. U.S. Congress, *Fair Labor Standards Act of 1938*, 75th Cong., 3d sess., Public Law no. 718, chap. 676, pp. 1060–1069.

8. U.S. Congress, *Fair Labor Standards Amendments of 1949*, 81st Cong., 1st sess. (Oct. 26, 1949), Public Law no. 393, chap. 736, pp. 910-920; *Fair Labor Standards Amendments of 1955*, 84th Cong., 2d sess. (Aug. 12, 1955), Public Law no. 381, chap. 867, pp. 711–712; *Fair Labor Standards Amendments of 1961*, 87th Cong., 2d sess. (May 5, 1961), Public Law no. 87–30, pp. 65–75; *Fair Labor Standards Amendments of 1966*, 89th Cong., 1st sess. (Sept. 23, 1966), Public Law no. 89–601, pp. 830–845; *Fair Labor Standards Amendments of 1974*, 93d Cong., 2d sess. (Apr. 8, 1974), Public Law no. 93–259, pp. 55–91; and *Fair Labor Standards Amendments of 1977*, 95th Cong., 1st sess. (Nov. 1, 1977), pp. 1245–1253.

9. The teenage minimum wage applies to workers 16 through 19 years of age. It can be paid for up to three months without government approval. It can also be paid for an additional three months if the employer is able to demonstrate to the U.S. Department of Labor that the workers are in an educational or training program.

10. The coverage for workers in low-wage industries rose even more dramatically than coverage for the entire work force, from approximately 10 percent in 1950 to 20 percent in 1962, 31 percent in 1967, 38 percent in 1974, and 44 percent in 1978, after which coverage among low-wage groups declined to 40 percent in 1988. Marvin H. Kosters, *Jobs and the Minimum Wage: The Effect of Changes in the Level and Pattern of Coverage*

(Washington, DC: American Enterprise Institute, Apr. 1989), pp. A–13 and A-15. For a summary of this study, see Marvin Kosters, "Minimum Wages: A Deeper Look at the '50s and '60s," *Wall Street Journal*, Oct. 19, 1987, p. 30.

CHAPTER 2

Initial Hostility

In the early 1970s, the *Times* editors were among the most vociferous of advocates for minimum-wage legislation, blatantly associating opponents to minimum-wage increases with the social politics of Marie Antoinette (Oct. 5, 1972). Such strong support for increases evolved gradually from much more analytical and sophisticated arguments against the minimum wage that were printed in the late 1930s.

Formative Years of Opposition

It was during the late 1930s that the proposal for the first minimum wage became a very lively political issue. Supporters, mainly union leaders, maintained that a federal minimum would protect low-wage workers from exploitation, particularly during depressions like the one that was still lingering at that time. Many other supporters argued that a minimum would increase workers' purchasing power, spur aggregate demand, and accelerate economic recovery. In spite of public interest in the subject, the *Times* editors were quiet on the federal minimum until late 1937. Their editorial attention to labor issues was focused on the growing union–management conflicts and on the political and economic fallout from the Wagner Act, recently passed to ease the unionization of workers.[1]

However, as the time approached for a vote on what was then called the wage and hour bill, the editors released a string of at least fifteen commentaries on what they foresaw to be the ill-conceived effects of the bill.[2] Nevertheless, in 1937, the editors made note of the perverse employment effects of the proposed minimum wage of 40 cents an hour included in the wage and hour bill, especially if agricultural workers were covered, given that "almost nowhere . . . do the average earnings of farm workers reach as high as this [$3.20 a day]." Then again, the editors stressed that if farm workers were not covered, then covered nonagricultural workers who were laid off because of the minimum wage could be expected to seek

13

employment in the exempted occupations. "The result is likely to be an even further depression of agricultural wage rates, already among the lowest in the country" (Dec. 9, 1937).

In their first 1938 editorial on the minimum wage, the *Times* editors sided squarely with the opponents, including many southern politicians, contending that the bill would act like a "tariff wall in the North against Southern goods," slowing both the expansion of indigenous southern industries and the movement of northern industry to the South (Feb. 15, 1938).[3] This would be the case because, the editors suggested, the minimum would wipe out any low-wage competitive advantage the South might have. They went on to reason that the proposed regional differential in the minimum ($13 a week for the North and $11 a week for the South) would not be an improvement over a uniform national wage. A differential might be "substantially greater or substantially less than that brought about by competitive conditions" (Feb. 15, 1938). In the former case, the North would be penalized by the minimum-wage law; in the latter case, the penalty would be against the South.

Besides, the editors observed, the "South" was not a clearly defined, separate region of the country for which one minimum wage could be established. If one wage differential could be justified on the grounds that the South would otherwise be penalized, then a whole network of differentials for various areas and industries of the economy could be justified.[4] In their support for leaving minimum wages to the states (half of whom had enacted such minimums by 1938, often determined administratively for individual industries), the editors wrote:

> These complexities point to the dilemma of a Federal Wage–Hour Bill. It disregards the differentials in wages between sections, States, large and small towns and different industries, and attempts to impose a single minimum, it must create profound disturbances. If the effort is made to write differentials into the bill, they must be extremely numerous and complex; there is no guarantee that they will be "right," and even if they should be "right" at the beginning, changes in conditions—in the price levels, in particular industries, or in particular sections—would soon make them wrong. If the attempt is made to escape this horn of the dilemma by allowing some commission or administrator to fix differentials at its discretion, then we create the arbitrariness and the day-to-day uncertainties of delegated power. (Feb. 15, 1938)[5]

Three months later, in May 1938, the *Times* editors went further and accused the bill's supporters of having ignored the federal government's experience with minimum-wage constraints devised by industries under the National Recovery Administration. The editors quoted from a 600-page report by a former director of research in the NRA:

> In fact, estimates have been made indicating that, directly or indirectly because of the minimum wage provisions of codes, about 500,000 Negro workers were on relief in 1934. . . . It has been demonstrated that a minimum wage benefits some classes, but imposes hardships on others. It definitely causes displacement of both the young inexperienced worker and the old one whose productivity has decreased. . . . The NRA plan definitely favored the highly mechanized units of industry at the expense of those employing larger proportions of hand labor.[6]

The editors' criticisms of minimum-wage supporters became even more pointed when they chided labor leaders John L. Lewis and William Green for "vying with each other to see which can make the stronger and more frequent statements in favor of the Federal Wage–Hour Bill," with the suggestion that these labor leaders were not so much concerned about the interests of workers as they were concerned about their own union membership drives. They stressed that a federal wage and hour bill can hike wages and shorten the workweek, but "it does not and cannot assure more employment. On the contrary, its tendency, if not counteracted by other forces, would be to reduce both individual annual income and employment," because the shorter workweek would mean a "smaller production of wealth." Also, "if wages of marginal workers are forced above the market value of the goods and services that those workers contribute to produce, they will no longer be hired." The editors then noted, with obvious regret, that labor leaders would be credited with increasing the wage and shortening the workweek but employers or "general conditions" would be blamed for reduced employment and loss of livelihood (May 10, 1938).

A week later, the *Times* editors once again damned the wage and hour legislation, arguing that none of its supporters had faced "with much realism" the unemployment problems the bill would likely cause. They took issue with supporters' claims that worker welfare could be enhanced by congressional fiat:

> We cannot make a man or woman worth a certain wage by declaring that he or she shall not be offered or shall not accept any less [than the proposed federal minimum wage]. We deprive such persons of whatever they could have earned, and we deprive the country of whatever services or goods they could have produced.

They noted that the House bill had been devised "without inquiry, without study, without any attempt to determine just how many persons will be affected by it, in what industries, in what sections, and how they will be affected." The bill just "blindly lays down its fixed minimum wages and minimum hours" (May 16, 1938).[7]

Daringly introducing the economist's technical concept of price "elasticity" of demand (or the responsiveness of employers to wage-rate changes) into the minimum-wage debate, in June 1938 the editors asked the question "Just how elastic is the demand for the services of workers?" Their own response drew on the calculations by Professor Paul Douglas from the University of Chicago (who later became a U.S. senator from Illinois) and Professor A. C. Pigou from Cambridge University, both of whom had concluded that the demand was relatively elastic with a coefficient between -3 and -4, which means that a 1 percent increase in the wage could be expected to lead to a 3 to 4 percent contraction in employment. Even if the true coefficient were proved to be somewhat less, the editors deduced that "it is still clear that arbitrary raising of wage rates above the productivity level is definitely adverse to the interests of labor and to the general welfare" (June 4, 1938).

No Letup after Passage

When in June 1938 passage of a wage and hour bill was practically assured by a congressional compromise including elimination of proposed wage differentials, the editors pulled back and tempered their hostility slightly, but only slightly:

> Common Sense and experience indicate that minimum-wage legislation is likely to be successful in proportion as its aims are modest. If it attempts to effect too sudden and too great a change in actual conditions, the harm it does must exceed the good. The new bill, when it becomes law, will represent one more major invasion by the Federal government of a field of regulation that should have been left to the States. (June 14, 1938)

In a news report carried in October 1938, during the week after the minimum wage went into effect, the *Times* appeared to validate the editors' worst fears. The reporter wrote:

> Almost at once the main objectives of the act were dramatized. The shutdown of some lumber mills and pecan-shelling establishments called attention to the fact that a minimum wage is

now set at 25 cents an hour for all covered establishments. The closed plants said they were unable to pay the minimum. A strike of Postal Telegraph wire operators brought into prominence the law's ban on a work week above forty-four hours except on payment of time and a half for overtime above that limit. The company and the operators were unable to agree on how the overtime problem was to be handled.[8]

By August, the editors' scorn for the wage and hour law had turned to mockery. They pointed out that while the hummingbird is among the most attractive birds in people's gardens, its "work-habits, according to all modern standards, are simply deplorable." Hummingbirds obviously violate the wage and hour law since they work "every hour of daylight. They extract no extra compensation for overtime. They don't knock off for lunch or even dinner." In addition, hummingbirds are "heartless exploiters of child labor," since they put their young to work when they are no "bigger than large bees" (Aug. 29, 1938).

The *Times* editors' sarcasm became caustic in November after the minimum wage had to be paid. They reported that Elmer Andrews, the newly appointed administrator of the Wage and Hour Act, already knew for a fact that the new law had caused the elimination of 30,000 to 50,000 jobs, mainly in the pecan-shelling, tobacco-stemming, lumber, and bagging industries — a point they made with some obvious satisfaction (Nov. 12, 1938).[9] What the editors could not believe is that the commissioner was blatantly willing to discount the employment consequences with the comment: "The significance of the lay-offs is ... reduced by the fact that a large share of the total consists of marginal and handicapped workers, whose position in the economic system has long been insecure." The commissioner went on to note that some of the laid-off marginal and handicapped workers "are already being replaced by more efficient workers able to earn the minimum hourly rate." For the editors, this validated the economic and human damage they predicted the law would cause (Nov. 12, 1938).

Nevertheless, the editors concluded their 1938 editorial blasts at the minimum wage with the slight concession that not all minimum-wage laws were necessarily harmful: "Minimum wage laws, within certain modest limits, can be helpful; pushed beyond those limits they can do more harm than good," which is reason enough that people must judge "social legislation, not merely by the nobility of the moral sentiments that inspired it, but by its actual economic consequences" (Nov. 12, 1938).

Notes

1. In 1936, the *Times* editors opposed efforts to generate "capacity production" by mandating a guaranteed minimum income of $3,600 a year for all workers (which, for a forty-hour week, amounts to $1.73 per hour). The editors complained that this "remedy puts the cart before the horse. A nation can never 'buy back' more than it produces. The primary way to increase American incomes is not to 'redistribute' more income than there is to go around, but to improve labor skills, machine efficiency and industrial organization—in short, to increase both individual earning power and national product." ("At least $3,600 a year," *New York Times*, Dec. 28, 1936 [editorial], p. 16)

   The editors' main arguments against the Wagner Act and what they considered the lack of balance in the developing labor laws are reflected in their lengthy labor editorials of 1937: "The Wagner Act," *New York Times*, Mar. 9, 1937 (editorial), p. 22; "One-Way Law," *New York Times*, Mar. 10, 1937 (editorial), p. 22; "Labor and the Law," *New York Times*, Mar. 16, 1937 (editorial), p. 22; "Collective Bargaining," *New York Times*, Mar. 26, 1937 (editorial), p. 20; "Legalizing the Sit-Down," *New York Times*, Mar. 30, 1937 (editorial), p. 22; "Resources Against Extremists," *New York Times*, June 27, 1937 (editorial), p. 20; "Special Privileges," *New York Times*, June 29, 1937 (editorial), p. 18; and "Government as Partisan," *New York Times*, Dec. 11, 1937 (editorial), p. 18.

2. The *Times* editors viewed the proposed restriction on the length of the workweek to forty hours (when many employees worked forty-eight or more) to be as pernicious as the minimum wage. See "The Question of Hours," *New York Times*, May 22, 1938 (editorial), sect. IV, p. 8; and "Working Hours," *New York Times*, May 26, 1938 (editorial), p. 24. The latter editorial argued that "implicit in the forty-hour week as a present objective is the fallacious idea that there is a fixed volume of production to be turned out, that there is therefore a fixed number of working man-hours to go around; and that, if individual hours are restricted, there must be a larger number of jobs." Such restrictions, however, could only reduce production and the country's standard of living.

3. The editors returned to the damage the wage and hour bill would do to the South in July 1938 ("'No. 1 Economic Problem,'" *New York Times*, July 7, 1938 [editorial], p. 18).

4. The editors noted that in 1929 (the last year for which data were available), there was a smaller difference in the average cost of manufacturing labor between South Carolina ($.23 an hour) and Virginia ($.36 an hour) than between Virginia and Maine ($.61 per hour) ("Wages 'North' and 'South'," *New York Times*, Feb. 15, 1938 [editorial], p. 24). The multitude of wage differentials effectively meant that the market should be left alone.

5. On another occasion, the *Times* editors noted that the federal government had recognized a need for differences in regional pay when it set up the Workers Progress Administration, including different pay scales for "four different classes of workers—skilled, intermediate skilled, pro-

fessional, and technical. The country is then divided into four different wage regions. Within each region itself there are five different geographical classifications depending on the size of populations of the towns." They then appealed to the words of President Roosevelt, who in 1937 had argued, in recommending the wage and hour law, "Even in the treatment of national problems there are geographical and industrial diversities which practical statesmanship cannot wholly ignore. Backward labor conditions and relatively progressive labor conditions cannot be completely assimilated and made uniform at one fell swoop without creating economic dislocations" ("Differential in Wages," *New York Times*, May 21, 1938 [editorial], p. 14).

In another editorial, they stressed that "those who oppose differentials in minimum wage rates usually confuse wage rates per hour with labor cost per unit of output—a very different thing. Europe, with low wage rates, is very much afraid of the competition of products of our mass production industries, where high wage rates are paid" ("'Principle' Vs. Substance," *New York Times*, June 8, 1938 [editorial], p. 22). On the issue of differentials, see also "House Vs. Senate Version," *New York Times*, May 25, 1938 [editorial], p. 22; and "The Wage Bill Compromise," *New York Times*, June 2, 1938 [editorial], p. 22; "'Standard Procedure,'" *New York Times*, June 3, 1938 [editorial], p. 20.

6. From Charles Frederick Roos, *NRA Economic Planning*, as quoted in "Minimum Wages and NRA," *New York Times*, May 27, 1938 [editorial], p. 16.

7. The editors returned to the problem of inadequate study of the effects of the minimum wage on several occasions, including "Legislating in the Dark," *New York Times*, May 24, 1938 [editorial], p. 18; "'Standard Procedure,'" *New York Times*, June 3, 1938 [editorial], p. 20; and "The Method of Reform," *New York Times*, June 5, 1938 [editorial], sect. IV, p. 8.

8. Louis Stark, "Wage and Hour Law Has Raised Many Questions," *New York Times*, Oct. 30, 1938 (news article), sect. IV, p. 3.

9. Andrews also estimated that the hours and the time-and-a-half pay provisions had the effect of increasing employment ("Wages, Hours Act Is Found Increasing Jobs; Andrews Reports Pay of 300,000 Affected," *New York Times*, Jan. 16, 1939 [news article], p. 1).

CHAPTER 3

The Years of Moderation and the First Turnaround

With political sentiment in the country solidly behind the wage and hour restrictions and with hope fading that the new labor market controls would be scrapped completely, the *Times* editors began to moderate their position. They were simply unable to find significant empirical support for their strongly held position.

Moderating Views

In their first editorial of 1939, the editors once again reminded minimum-wage supporters that they should have judged the efficacy of a federal minimum wage by investigating the individual states' experiences with minimum-wage laws (Apr. 27, 1939). As it was, the federal minimum had, along with disastrous hurricanes and a reduction in the quota for Puerto Rican sugar that year, "disorganized" the Puerto Rican economy to such an extent that the Roosevelt administration and other minimum-wage supporters were considering a special exclusion for Puerto Rico (along with the Virgin Islands) (Apr. 27, 1939).[1] The editors suggested the process of making exceptions could easily degenerate into "discrimination and political favoritism" and that any case for making Puerto Rico a special exception should be taken as a case for changing the nature of the system (July 21, 1939). However, as an alternative to the wage and hour law, the editors said special federal industrial commissions (which already existed) should be delegated the authority to adjust wage and hour restrictions freely to individual circumstances, a recommendation made without overt concern that such a process would also degenerate into "discrimination and political favoritism" (Apr. 27, 1939). In their July 1939 editorial, the editors not only repeated their recommendation but added that the wage and hour law needed a "thorough-going revision" because it had been promoted in the name of low-wage, unskilled workers but was affecting the country's entire labor market through restrictions on hours worked and overtime paid.[2]

In 1940, the *Times* editors advocated the inclusion of agricultural workers under the wage and hour law, but not in the name of equity or humanity (as they would argue in the 1950s and 1960s). Rather, they maintained that the best laws do not discriminate and therefore are not subject to political manipulation. "If we are to have such a [wage–hour] law," the editors wrote, "it ought to apply to all such labor to the greatest extent practicable. There is no excuse for exempting agricultural labor except the sheer administrative difficulty of covering some of it." This theme prevailed in all of their commentaries of 1940, after the minimum wage had gone to 30 cents an hour (Apr. 12, 1940).[3]

In most of their editorials during 1938, 1939, and 1940, the *Times* editors opposed the initial wage and hour law and either opposed or supported revisions based on appeals to principle in the development of labor policy. However, perhaps out of frustration that may have come with consistently being on the losing side, the editors appeared to break with that tradition at least once, suggesting that in the debate over an appropriate reconstruction of the wage–hour law, "the real question is not theoretical but practical: The problem is to determine in different lines what length working week will lead to maximum production while safeguarding the health and general welfare of the workers." They then endorsed an increase in the workweek restriction to forty-eight hours because a study by the Twentieth Century Fund had found that "maximum output per worker lies [in a workweek] somewhere between forty-eight and sixty hours a week for most occupations" (Apr. 5, 1944).

The *Times* editors never came back to the minimum wage during the height of the war years, in spite of various efforts to speed up the increase in the minimum to 40 cents scheduled for 1945 and to raise it to 65 or even 72 cents.[4] The workweek and the time-and-a-half provisions in the Wage and Hour Act, which the editors saw as equivalent to wage controls and similar to minimum-wage rates, were far more pressing concerns. They reasoned that in a time of war the country should do everything possible to expand the availability of both military and consumer goods. The forty-hour week had created an "artificial scarcity" that could give rise to inflation or, in the editors' vernacular, "compulsory inflation."[5] They noted that the original intent of the workweek limitation in the Wage and Hour Act was to "spread the work," but in a time of war when much manpower is drained off by the military, noted:

It is an absurd contradiction to keep this penalty rate for overtime above forty hours and then to compel employers to work their men more than forty hours. It is like putting a fine on speeding and then forcing motorists to speed so that the fine could be collected. (Feb. 11, 1943)

And, the editors observed, the fine grows with the pay rate of workers. If a worker is paid $1 an hour, "the law insists that he be paid 50 cents an hour extra for time over forty hours; if he is getting only 40 cents an hour, the law insists he be paid 20 cents an hour for time over forty hours," a requirement that is bound to lead to "economic absurdities" (June 12, 1942). After the war, the editors repeatedly pressed the federal government to get out of the business of setting wages and prices—matters, they reasoned, that should be left to the marketplace (see, e.g., Jan. 4, 1946).

The *Times* editors launched a frontal assault on the minimum wage early in 1946, when they charged that the Truman administration, which had recently proposed increasing the minimum wage from 40 to 65 cents an hour, had not given the issue "serious study" to determine how many workers were earning the minimum wage and what the damage would be to jobs if the proposed new minimum were adopted (Mar. 27, 1946). The editors were soon taken to task by Metcalfe Walling, administrator of the Wage and Hour Division of the Labor Department, who claimed that government studies showed the impact would be minimal. He estimated that less than 2 million workers would be covered by the summer of 1945, and the cost of raising everyone to the 65-cent minimum would increase the nation's total payroll by only 2 percent. He called attention to the fact that ever since the first state minimum-wage law was passed in Massachusetts in 1912, opponents had raised the "hoary" specter of job losses but stated, "There is no historical evidence that any appreciable number of workers had been refused employment because of minimum-wage requirements."[6]

The editors printed their rejoinder to the administrator on the same day. They acknowledged that "estimates" (the quotation marks are the editors') of the coverage of the minimum wage did exist, but they quickly added that the government had recognized that the statistical methods used to develop the estimates made them, in the words of a government publication, "subject to a considerable margin of error." Citing an article in the *Harvard Business Review* by Professor John V. Van Sickle, the editors stressed that 42 percent of the manufacturing workers in Tennessee earned less than the minimum. In apparel, 43 percent of Tennessee workers were paid less than 50 cents an hour and 93 percent less than 65 cents an hour.

The editors supported their claim that workers in the South would be disadvantaged by the new minimum with data that showed that, in the West, 1 percent of lumber workers earned less than 65 cents an hour but that in the South nearly 90 percent of lumber workers earned less than 65 cents an hour. They suggested it was incredulous that anyone in the administration could argue that the proposed 62.5 percent increase in the minimum could be absorbed readily, without significant adverse employment effects, by American businesses: "To believe that such an increase can be achieved overnight by a mere stroke of the pen, without any bad consequences on production and employment, is to have a sublime faith in legislative fiat." If the administration truly felt the employment effects would be inconsequential, then "why not forget 'hoary' apprehensions entirely and make the hourly minimum $1, $2, $5, or what not?" (Apr. 13, 1946).

The political press for a 75-cent minimum wage with expanded coverage continued into 1948 with the full support of the Truman administration. In spite of Truman's previously announced support for a minimum-wage increase, the *Times* editors found much to appreciate in his midyear economic report for 1948. The editors praised the president for recommending an agenda that stressed, in general, the "time-tested policies associated with what has come to be referred to as the American way"—mainly, policies that encouraged business and did not rely on "'compensating' government activities." They said the report "breathes the wholesome spirit of free enterprise."[7]

The First Turnaround

When the issue of the minimum wage returned to the political spotlight, the editors' widely and frequently advertised devotion to free-market principles began to give way in the postwar years to a more practical concern: What had experience with the minimum wage over the preceding twelve years actually wrought? By 1950, the editors' published views on the minimum wage had for the first time turned dramatically, presumably because of data-based arguments. The day after the new 75-cent minimum became effective in late January 1950, the editors started their first minimum-wage editorial in two years in a matter-of-fact manner. They noted that the new minimum wage would affect the incomes of 1.3 to 1.5 million workers but that the new minimum would not raise wages by 87.5 percent as the jump from 40 to 75 cents an hour seemed to imply (Jan. 28, 1950). According to data provided by the Truman Labor Depart-

24

ment, which the editors did not question, the average pay of the "substandard" employees was already at 60 to 70 cents per hour.[8]

At this point, the editors almost completely abandoned their opposition to the 75-cent minimum. Their only expressed concern was that the "sound humanitarian and social concept" of the minimum wage be protected from "its critics and from its more ardent supporters" (Jan. 28, 1950) (who were already pushing for a $1 minimum).[9] Without acknowledging they had been staunch "critics" two years earlier or that they were about to deny the validity of carefully crafted contentions made repeatedly in their earlier editorials, the editors added:

> None of the dire results predicted have materialized from the 1938 Act, and the present legislation merely brings the latter [minimum-wage rate] into line with wage and living-cost realities of today. So long as the principle is confined to its original social objectives of protecting the worker from exploitation and assuring him a living wage there is no reason to doubt that it will continue to justify itself in the future as it has in the past.

The editors' only expressed fear was that "however admirable within these limits [which were left unspecified], [a minimum-wage increase] could defeat its own ends and nullify its beneficial effects if people should permit themselves to be convinced that it represented a triumph for the so-called 'purchasing power' principle of economics" (Jan. 28, 1950).[10]

Why the editorial shift? A turnover of key editorial writers may or may not account for the turnaround on the minimum wage. It is important to note that Henry Hazlitt, a staunch free-market philosopher and *Times* editorial writer, left the paper in 1946 (after working there since 1934). However, the editorials in 1948, after Hazlitt had left, were as adamantly opposed to the minimum wage as in 1946. Clearly, the turnaround cannot be attributed to changes at the top of the *Times* organization. Arthur Hays Sulzberger was president and publisher from 1935 until 1961. Julius Ochs Adler, vice president and general manager in 1950, had held that position from at least the passage of the first federal minimum wage in 1938.

The editors left the minimum-wage issue alone for the next three years. However, in 1953, they fortified their support of the federal minimum-wage law by complimenting James Mitchell, newly confirmed secretary of labor in the Eisenhower administration, for revealing "a sensitive understanding of social values when he advocated amending the minimum-wage law to cover millions of wage-earners who have no federal protection against substandard wages. This should have long been a

Congressional must" (Nov. 19, 1953). In past years, the editors had advocated extending the coverage of the minimum, but mainly to prevent discrimination and political favoritism. Now, they favored the extension primarily on moral or humanitarian grounds, a motivation they recognized could not be followed without acknowledged limits.

In these early years of support for the minimum wage, the *Times* editors appeared to want a "sensible minimum" (a theme, expressed under changing rubrics, to which they would return time and again over the ensuing three decades). They also appeared to adopt a widely expressed theory among minimum-wage supporters that relatively "small" mandated increases in the wages of "substandard" workers would have little or no effect on employment, but, beyond some point, an increase would make the cost of labor uncompetitive and jobs would be lost.[11]

That is to say, the editors and others may have thought of "exploitative" and "unconscionable" employers of substandard workers as monopsonists (employers with sufficient market power to suppress their workers' wages below competitive levels), a theoretical refinement of basic labor market theory that was formalized in 1946 by then University of Minnesota Professor George Stigler.[12] Such employers are able to pay wages below competitive levels by simply reducing their demand for labor (equating monopsonists' marginal cost of labor with labor's marginal value).[13] As long as the minimum-wage increase is no greater than that which would place employers on their demand curves, employment will not contract (indeed, it will increase up to a point). However, job losses will mount once employers are forced by minimum-wage increases to move farther up their labor-demand curves.

Theory aside, the *Times* editors revealed more explicitly in a 1955 editorial why they may have become backers of both an increase to the minimum wage and an expansion of its coverage. In earlier years, they had called for an exhaustive study of the effects of minimum-wage increases, which they must have thought, given their hostility toward minimum wages, would include significant job losses. In 1954, they got the study for which they had sought so vigorously at first to fortify their previous opposition and later in 1954, to reinforce their newfound support. According to the editors, the Labor Department had undertaken a "thorough study" of the 35 cent (or 87.5 percent) increase in the minimum wage in 1950 on low-wage industries and had found that the increase had "no marked effect either on employment or business mortality—in spite of the dire predictions of opponents of the change" (June 14, 1955). Thus, while the Labor Department study was not actually an unqualified endorsement of the 1950 increase in the minimum wage,[14] the *Times* editors reasoned that the proposed 25 cent (or 33.3 percent) increase, which would raise the nation's total wage bill by less than .7 percent, should be less of a problem than the 1950 increase, a position fortified three weeks later by six university economists in a letter to the *Times* editors.[15]

The editors' switch on the minimum wage may be explained by a number of considerations, not the least of which is that the six economists who wrote the *Times* in support of the proposed minimum-wage increase were not alone among academics. At the time, the minimum wage had not been a major focus of scholarly articles in the economic literature. Only fourteen articles on the topic had appeared in major scholarly journals and collections of economic papers between 1938 and 1955 (a figure that represents less than 10 percent of the total articles on the minimum wage that would be in print in similar works up to 1984).[16] In addition, one of the most widely used economics textbooks, the second edition of Paul A. Samuelson's *Economics* published in 1951, carried only a passing reference to the existence of the minimum wage and offered no commentary on its consequences.[17] In a textbook that was also in widespread use in the early 1950s, George Leland Bach did take up the topic of the minimum wage, explained how, theoretically, it could reduce employment, but he concluded the analysis with an expression of doubt in the economic theory he was presenting. "Whether it really works this way in any appreciable number of cases is not clear from the evidence."[18]

President Eisenhower's Council of Economic Advisors, headed by Arthur Burns, a former Columbia University professor and a widely recognized conservative economist, had endorsed in the 1954 *Economic Report of the President* both an increase in the minimum wage by an unspecified amount (to be determined after review of the Labor Department's study on the 1950 increase) and a substantial expansion of the coverage of the minimum wage.[19] The Eisenhower economists reasoned that the coverage needed to be extended to "millions" of additional workers to protect those already covered from suffering a competitive disadvantage caused by the minimum wage.[20] Burns and his council associates maintained that political demands for an increase in the minimum wage should be moderated, however, because

> a minimum does not protect the inadequately rewarded
> worker if it is too low. On the other hand, it may not benefit
> him if it is so high as to push up the whole scaffolding of wages
> and of costs of doing business, thus leading either to inflation
> of prices and the worker's own living costs, or to elimination

of the less efficient employers and workers. Yet the ability of the employer to absorb a high minimum wage is limited.[21]

The *Times* editors quoted approvingly the economists' conclusion:

> While minimum-wage laws do not get at the fundamental causes of poverty, they can make a useful contribution to its reduction. Recognizing that an increase of the minimum now provided by Federal law and expansion of its coverage are desirable, the exact nature and timing of these changes must be worked out with a view to the best interests of the economy.[22]

Following in step with Burns and his associates, the *Times* editors concluded that the added labor cost could be accommodated by businesses because labor productivity had risen by 20 percent since the last minimum increase.[23]

Perhaps even more important, the *Times* editors took to the offensive and endorsed the contention of many northern industrialists that "a substantial increase [in the minimum wage] will reduce 'unfair' regional competition based on lower wage costs in the South" (June 14, 1955); more generally, as one letter writer indicated, the increase will fulfill a basic purpose of the original minimum-wage law, which is to "prevent the cutthroat competition of unscrupulous firms which pay the lowest possible wages they can legally get away with."[24] The *Times* editors accepted, or just reiterated, their letter writer's basic position when they defended an earlier minimum-wage editorial calling for an increase in the minimum to $1 an hour (just after the 75-cent minimum went into effect) and for universal coverage:[25]

> Let us note, in the first place, that the principal purpose of the minimum wage is to protect the worker who is at or near the subsistence wage level from being exploited by being pushed below the subsistence level in order that marginal and frequently inefficient proprietors can survive. Those who first advocated it were thinking particularly in terms of women and younger workers. (Apr. 14, 1956)

Thus, without recognizing or acknowledging the turnaround in their editorial position, the editors repudiated one of their favorite arguments used in opposition to the first minimum-wage laws: the minimum wage is designed, with political forethought, to be anticompetitive—more specifically, anti-South, antiwomen, and anti–young workers—an admission that for years may have fueled opposition to additional minimum-wage increases.[26]

The *Times* editors' switch from opposition to support of the minimum-wage concept was completed in 1956 when they endorsed a proposal that New York state's minimum wage be increased to $1 an hour, arguing that all New York workers, not just those covered by the federal minimum, "deserve the equal protection of the laws" (Mar. 12, 1956).

In the late 1950s, the New York State minimum wage had become a maze of ten different wages for ten industries, each of which had been established by state "tripartite" wage boards (composed of representatives of management, workers, and government) that supposedly based their minimum-wage decisions on their specific industries' needs and problems as determined by investigations. Adjustments in industry-specific minimum wages had become both time consuming and expensive, facts widely recognized by proponents and opponents of state-determined wage floors.[27] During the 1930s and 1940s, the *Times* editors had at times argued for industry-specific federal minimum wages. In 1959, however, they sided with proponents of a uniform state minimum, contending that the observed "evils" of differential minimums would be "wiped out" by a flat statewide minimum. The editors expressed concern that the proposed 50-cent increase in the state minimum might be too high, given the existing federal minimum wage (Nov. 19, 1959) and that the effects of the state minimum wage were worthy of greater study by "an impartial agency, skilled in public and business administration" (Dec. 19, 1959). Nevertheless, they endorsed an increase in the state minimum, rationalizing that a then recent "grim outbreak of youth crimes in New York" might be tied to low wages in the state, especially among Puerto Rican and black teenagers (Sept. 26, 1959).

In 1960, when raising New York City's minimum wage to $1.25 was proposed, the *Times* editors cited new evidence for their support. They noted that at the time an estimated 250,000 people were on public assistance in the city but that as many as 350,000 not on the welfare roles had incomes that were "substandard, a bare minimum for health and safety." Increasing the city's minimum wage by an additional 50 cents would provide "real public assistance to the taxpayers in the town" by lowering welfare expenditures by as much as $1 million (Feb. 22, 1960).

In February 1961, the editors endorsed President Kennedy's proposed three-step increase in the minimum wage from $1 to $1.25 and then added that the coverage of the minimum should be extended beyond the Kennedy proposal (Feb. 9, 1962). They were especially concerned that farmworkers would be left uncovered. (However, they accepted limits to the extension of coverage set by the interstate "commerce clause" of the Constitution [Apr. 23, 1961].) They once again suggested that "evil effects" of the minimum wage had been greatly exaggerated in the past, and they claimed, without support, that because most of the covered workers would be involved in "production for domestic use . . . there would be little or no adverse effect on our competitive position" (Feb. 9, 1961).

A month later, editors argued that helping those "unable to protect themselves is a long-accepted and necessary function of the Federal Government" and that instituting the proposed 25-cent increase in the minimum would go a long way toward fulfilling that important govern-ment function. They returned to what had by that time become a favorite theme of theirs, that previous claims of widespread business failures and job losses were not supported by statistics: "For example, in 1959 the Wage and Hour Administrator informed Congress that of the 2,100,000 employ-ees affected by the 1956 increase in the minimum to $1, less than 2,000 were discharged or otherwise adversely affected" (Mar. 21, 1961).

The editors went further, claiming (without reference to source):

> Surveys have shown that a higher minimum in low-wage communities has actually stimulated, rather than depressed, employment, and has stimulated it not only far beyond the national average but to a greater degree in the specific indus-tries affected by the new minimum than in the industries not so affected.

They then discounted foreign competition as a threat on the grounds that "wages in most of our export industries are already above the minimum, and in other cases the projected increase would have but a minor effect on the sale price of the product" (Feb. 9, 1961). In follow-up editorials on the Kennedy minimum-wage proposal, the editors repeated their claims, still without substantiation, that adverse employment effects would most likely be minuscule, if detectable at all, especially since many workers would remain outside the law's coverage.[28]

Notes

1. See also "A New Dispute in Congress," *New York Times*, July 21, 1939 (editorial), p. 18; and M. B. Thomas, "Puerto Rico's Plight," *New York Times*, May 16, 1939 (letter to the editor), p. 22.

2. To reduce the adverse impact of the wage–hour law, Commissioner Andrews recommended that the hours and overtime restrictions apply only to workers earning more than $200 a month. However, with unusual candor in explaining his change of mind, which the *Times* editors deplored, Andrews gave union opposition to the change as his reason: "Organized labor has done such a swell job of fighting battles for me that I think it would be unethical for me to press that amendment if they are opposed to it" (as quoted by the *Times* editors in "Mr. Andrews Changes His Mind," *New York Times*, July 22, 1939 [editorial], p. 14.) From a following editorial, it appears that Andrews may have lost his job because of his frank admission ("Andrews Out, Fleming In," *New York Times*, Oct. 19, 1939 [editorial], p. 22).

3. See also "Wage–Hour Amendments," *New York Times*, Apr. 25, 1940 (editorial), p. 22; "Wage–Hour Amendments," *New York Times*, Apr. 29, 1938 (editorial), p. 14; "Time for Responsibility," *New York Times*, May 6, 1940 (editorial), p. 16.

4. The editors did comment on a proposal to increase the minimum wage to 72 cents late in the war ("Wage Policy," *New York Times*, July 24, 1945 [editorial], p. 22). Their main expressed concern was that in light of the continuing "large volume of excess purchasing power," the proposed wage hike would accelerate the "wage–price spiral" (ibid.).

5. See "The Forty-Hour Week," *New York Times*, June 14, 1942 (editorial), sect. IV, p. 10; "The War Against Inflation," *New York Times*, Sept. 28, 1942 (editorial), p. 16; "A 37-Hour Week," *New York Times*, Oct. 27, 1942 (editorial), p. 24; "A 33-Hour Week," *New York Times*, Oct. 30, 1942 (editorial), p. 18; "The 48-Hour Week," *New York Times*, Nov. 20, 1942 (editorial), p. 22; "Compulsory Inflation," *New York Times*, Feb. 12, 1943 (editorial), p. 18; and "'Curing' a Labor Shortage," *New York Times*, Jan. 16, 1945 (editorial), p. 18.

6. Metcalfe Walling, "Wage Studies Are Outlined: Administrator Sees No Discouragement of Employment in Proposed Rate," *New York Times*, Apr. 13, 1946 (letter to the editor), p. 16. The National Consumers League believes that its first secretary, Florence Kelley, proposed the first federal minimum wage in 1910 (Vera M. Waltman, "To Raise the Minimum Wage," *New York Times*, May 6, 1959 [letter to the editor], p. 38).

7. "A Reassuring Report," *New York Times*, July 12, 1948 (editorial), p. 26.

8. The editors may have also been impressed with then Senator Claude Pepper (D-FL), sponsor of the Senate version of the minimum-wage increase, who estimated that the new minimum would cost U.S. businesses $300 million, or raise the country's total wage bill by about 0.5 percent, a point that caused the editors to deduce "that the law will not be burdensome to any industry" (as quoted in Louis Stark, "Conferees

Agreed on 75C Basic Pay; Congress Acts Soon," *New York Times*, Oct. 15, 1949 [news article], p. 1).

9. Anthony Leviero, "Truman Signs Pay Raise Bill; Drive for $1 Minimum Starts," *New York Times*, Oct. 27, 1949 (news article), p. 1.

10. The "'purchasing power' principle of economics" was left undefined. From previous commentaries by advocates of the minimum wage, the reference might be to the theory that the cost effects of the minimum wage would be offset by the increase in aggregate demand due to the increase in the income of minimum-wage workers.

11. See the extended commentary of L. Metcalfe Walling (administrator of the Wage and Hour Division, U.S. Department of Labor), *New York Times*, Apr. 13, 1946 (letter to the editor), p. 16.

12. George Stigler, "The Economics of the Minimum Wage," *American Economic Review, 36* (June 1946), pp. 358–365.

13. A discussion of the way monopsonists will be affected by a minimum wage is provided in Chapter 8.

14. The Labor Department study did note that the 1950 minimum wage increased average worker wages significantly (by as much as 20 percent) and concluded, in general, that "the 75-cent rate had only very minor determinable effects on employment and other nonwage variables in the five low-wage manufacturing industries surveyed" (U.S. Department of Labor, Wage and Hour and Public Contracts Divisions, *Results of the Minimum-Wage Increase of 1950: Economic Effects in Selected Low-Wage Industries and Establishments*, [Washington, DC: U.S. Government Printing Office, Aug. 1954], p. 19). However, the Labor Department report also saw fit to add numerous caveats on interpretations of their findings (e.g., their findings may have been greatly influenced by the economic upswing spurred by the Korean conflict) and to conclude, "In Southern sawmills over the short run, employment fell 2 percent; some mills indicated the higher minimum forced layoffs of less able, usually older workers" (ibid., p. 13). However, the Labor Department attributed the fall in employment, without benefit of regression analysis, to many other factors, e.g., the weather (ibid.).

15. The university economists who signed the letter supporting the minimum wage were Richard A. Lester, Leland J. Gordon, Elizabeth Brandeis, Edwin E. Witte, Mabel Newcomer, and Seymour E. Harris ("Minimum Wage Rise: Studies Said to Reveal Favorable Results of Legislation," *New York Times*, July 8, 1955 [letter to the editor], p. 22). After citing additional data reported by the Labor Department, the six economists charged supporters from the U.S. Chamber of Commerce with basing their opposition to a minimum increase on "long-run classical theory" and claimed: "Minimum-wage experience clearly demonstrates that abstract and mechanistic reasoning can lead one to completely erroneous conclusions. Time after time during the past fifty years practical results have proved the unsoundness of dire predictions concerning the consequences of legal minimums when the predictions were based on a doctrinaire position" (ibid.).

16. In 1984, there were at least 189 articles in print in major economics journals and collections of articles, which hardly covers all public policy discussions of the effects of the minimum wage. This number is based on the author's count of minimum-wage articles listed in the American Economic Association, *Index of Economic Articles in Journals and Collected Volumes*, all volumes between 1925 and 1984 (Homewood, IL: Irwin). The *Index* covers journals that the selection committee of the American Economics Association considers "most helpful to research workers and teachers of economics" (ibid., 1988, p. xvii). Part of the growth in economics articles on the minimum wage between 1940 and 1970 can be attributed to an almost doubling of the number of journals covered, from 89 to 182. However, the growth in the number of articles on the minimum wage after the 1970s is much greater than the growth in the journals covered. The journals covered by the *Index* increased by 22 percent, from 182 in 1970 to 222 in 1984. However, the number of minimum-wage articles printed during the 1970 to 1984 period was double the number printed in all years prior to 1970.

17. Paul A. Samuelson, *Economics: An Introductory Analysis*, 2d ed. (New York: McGraw-Hill, 1951), p. 203.

18. George Leland Bach, *Economics: An Introduction to Analysis and Policy* (Englewood Cliffs, NJ: Prentice-Hall, 1954).

19. Executive Office of the President, Council of Economic Advisors, *Economic Report of the President: 1954* (Washington, DC: U.S. Government Printing Office, January 28, 1954), pp. 100–102. The other two members of the Council of Economic Advisors under Burns were Neil H. Jacoby and Walter W. Stewart.

20. Ibid., p. 101.

21. Ibid.

22. *Economic Report of the President: 1954*, p. 102, as quoted in "Report Cautious on Minimum Wage: It Favors Increase and Wider Coverage But Says Timing Is a Major Factor," *New York Times*, Jan. 29, 1954, (news article), p. 9. In 1955, President Eisenhower recommended an increase in the minimum wage to 90 cents an hour, reasoning that the increase in the cost of living since the last minimum-wage increase would justify a minimum wage of 86 cents. Cabinet members decided not to go higher than 90 cents because they intended to seek an expansion in the coverage of the minimum wage, mainly affecting southern industries ("Transcript of the Presidential News Conference," *New York Times*, Apr. 28, 1955 [text], p. 12).

23. "Report Cautious on Minimum Wage: It Favors Increase and Wider Coverage But Says Timing Is a Major Factor," *New York Times*, Jan. 29, 1954 (news article), p. 9.

24. Joseph Bernstein, "Benefits of the Minimum Wage," *New York Times*, Mar. 17, 1956 (letter to the editor), p. 18.

25. The editors wrote in March 1956 that only 2.1 million of the nation's 65 million wage earners would be affected by the new 75-cent minimum and that "it is not only unfair but inhuman not to give all our low in-

come workers the equal protection of the laws" ("New Floor for Wages," *New York Times*, Mar. 1, 1956 [editorial], p. 32). The editors later endorsed George Meany's proposal to extend coverage to an additional 9.5 million workers, mainly in large department and chain stores, logging firms, theaters, motels, real estate and finance, dry cleaners, and laundries, as well as farmworkers, workers processing farm products and seafood, and outside salespeople ("Wage Floor Extensions," *New York Times*, May 14, 1956 [editorial], p. 24). The editors later pulled back, for mainly practical political reasons, and endorsed the more modest extension of coverage recommended by the Eisenhower administration. President Eisenhower and Secretary of Labor James Mitchell recommended extending coverage to about 2 million employees of all firms doing business across state lines with a worth of $1 million annually and employing 100 or more workers ("Wage Floor Extensions," *New York Times*, Feb. 28, 1957 [editorial], p. 26).

26. In the late 1960s, the *Wall Street Journal* editors condemned the passage of the 1966 increase in the minimum wage by declaring, as the *Times* editors had done before, that the passage of the national minimum wage was deliberately designed by northerners as an anti-South measure and that the minimum wage acted like a "protective tariff" that would "dictate the terms on which Southern labor could compete" ("The Economic War Between the States," *Wall Street Journal*, Sept. 26, 1966, p. 18). The *Times* editors, however, may have accepted the minimum wage as a device for suppressing competition because it had previously accepted the legal reasoning of Justice Stone that was included in a 1956 letter to the editors: "A wage is not always the resultant of free bargaining between employers and employees . . . it may be one forced upon employees by their economic necessities and on employers by the most ruthless of their competitors . . . a wage insufficient to support the worker does not visit its consequences upon him alone; it may affect profoundly the entire economic structure of society, and, in any case, it casts on every taxpayer and on Government itself the burden of solving the problems of poverty, subsistence, health and morals of large numbers in the community. Because of their nature and extent these are public problems" (as quoted by Elizabeth S. Magee [Secretary general, National Consumers League], "To Extend the Minimum Wage," *New York Times*, Mar. 7, 1956 [letter to the editor], p. 32).

27. For contrasting positions on New York's minimum wages, see David Segal, "To Raise the Minimum Wage," *New York Times*, Dec. 12, 1959 (letter to the editor), p. 22; and Ralph C. Gross, "Minimum Wage Questioned," *New York Times*, Nov. 28, 1959 (letter to the editor), p. 20.

28. "Minimum Wage Compromise," *New York Times*, May 2, 1961 (editorial), p. 36; "Minimum Wage in the Senate," *New York Times*, Apr. 13, 1961 (editorial), p. 34; "The Minimum Wage," *New York Times*, Apr. 23, 1961 (editorial), sect. IV, p. 12; and "A Dollar and Up an Hour," *New York Times*, Sept. 5, 1961 (editorial), p. 34.

CHAPTER 4

The Search for a
Sensible Wage Policy

Having turned from opposition to support of the minimum wage, the editors at the *New York Times* remained concerned that political leaders would not recognize the limits of their economic powers to help low-income workers. They were especially concerned that state and local political leaders would not recognize that New York state and city might lose a significant portion of their economic bases if state and city minimum-wage policies were not pursued with caution.

Newfound Opposition to City and State Minimums

In 1961, Mayor Wagner had signed a New York City ordinance requiring all city contractors to pay their employees at least $1.50 an hour, at a time when the federal minimum was $1.15 an hour. The ordinance did not impose a minimum wage on all city businesses, just on those that did business with the city. The *Times* editors endorsed the limited ordinance in January 1962 on the grounds that the city was "moving downhill in relative wage standing because of the predominance of the city's manufacturing industries of small, highly competitive businesses, which often take advantage of the plentiful supply of Puerto Rican and Negro labor." The law, according to the editors, was a "wholesome evocation of municipal conscience"; the city had a duty to "fortify decent labor standards for those at the bottom of the economic ladder" (Jan. 1, 1962).

However, when the mayor proposed that the city adopt a minimum wage of $1.50 an hour for all city businesses, the editors went on the attack with a series of five editorials between August and October 1962, including arguments that stood in sharp contrast to the position they had taken on the mayor's required minimum wage for municipal contractors. The editors simply articulated strong economic explanations for their new opposition on the municipal (but not federal) minimum wage. For the first time, the editors acknowledged that city jobs would be lost if a higher municipal minimum were adopted (although it would be years before they would concede the possibility of significant job losses under the federal minimum). While the existing low wages remained a "community disgrace," "the only thing wrong with this 'remedy' [the municipal minimum wage] is that it would eliminate jobs as well as low wages." This is because New York City is not an "economic island"—the loss of manufacturing jobs to Pennsylvania, New Jersey, and the South would be "vastly accelerated." "No legislative fiat," the editors wrote, "can compel employers with little capital investment and limited need for highly skilled labor to stay in New York if it pushes its minimum so much above those prevailing elsewhere." As noted, seven months earlier the editors had suggested that low-wage, unskilled Puerto Rican and Negro workers would be the chief beneficiaries of the municipal wage boost; now, they were contending that these two groups would be the "chief sufferers" (Jan. 1, 1962).

In an August 1962 follow-up commentary, the editors accused the mayor of "asking the New York City Council to sign the death warrant for the jobs of thousands of workers in highly competitive industries, whose employers will not hesitate to move to other areas where the legal wage floor is lower." The proposed ordinance would increase the city's welfare burden and at the same time shrink its industrial tax base (Aug. 20, 1962). In September, the editors cited the city's loss since 1954 of 5,000 factories (a loss of more than $1 billion in city business). The proposed wage bill (which was at the time of the editorial scheduled to take effect on the upcoming election eve), they said, would only expand the "mortality list." They implored the city fathers to recognize that New York businesses do not have a "guaranteed market" and that competition is "regional, national and global—as close as Yonkers and Jersey City, and as remote as Tokyo and Hong Kong" (Sept. 18, 1962).

After the measure was approved and signed into law, the editors begrudgingly implied that the mayor had endorsed the minimum wage as a political ploy, knowing that the ordinance probably would be declared unconstitutional (which it was) (Oct. 25, 1962). That legal setback did not deter the city council, however, from proposing, in 1964, another municipal minimum wage, which the *Times* editors called "delusive and cruel" because it would speed up automation (June 25, 1964).[1] The new 1964 municipal minimum also was declared unconstitutional (Aug. 26, 1964).

The *Times* editors employed the same arguments they had used

36

against the municipal minimum wage in opposing the increase in the New York state minimum when it was being considered in 1965. They maintained that the proposed $1.50 state minimum, which would be 25 cents an hour above the federal minimum at the time, would accelerate the exodus of New York industry to Pennsylvania, New Jersey, and the South, and that the state minimum would be harmful to Puerto Ricans and Negroes, especially to teenagers in those minorities. The editors admonished state legislators to "concentrate on the demand for a higher federal minimum wage" and to press for "more tripartite wage boards" to whom could be delegated the task of setting minimum-wage rates for those industries "not directly affected by out-of-state competition and that do have the capacity to pay more without curtailing employment or forcing enterprises into bankruptcy" (Mar. 24, 1965). When Governor Rockefeller vetoed the state minimum-wage increase, the editors applauded (Apr. 19, 1965).

Continued Support for the Federal Minimum

By mid-1965, the federal minimum wage had reemerged as a contested political issue, but during that year the *Times* editors began to recognize the potential for employment loss if the federal minimum were to be set arbitrarily too high, without a reasonable foundation in statistical studies on the issue. Indeed, they chided President Johnson, who had told Congress to do what they thought best on the minimum wage, for defaulting on his "responsibility to provide Congress with guidance it had a right to expect from the Bureau of Labor Statistics." Without employment studies, the editors maintained that "guesswork had become the Congressional guidepost, and no one can be sure how much harm the proposed minimum might do to those who find it hardest to get and hold jobs" (Aug. 5, 1965).

By 1966, the requisite studies had been done, and the *Times* editors sided with President Johnson's Secretary of Labor Willard Wirtz, who claimed in his call for a higher minimum that the previous increase had neither hurt employment nor accelerated inflation (Mar. 14, 1966). In doing so, the editors stood against the president's Council of Economic Advisors, who had publicly split with the labor secretary on the increase mainly on the grounds that it might be inflationary (Feb. 22, 1966).

In September 1966, in response to President Johnson's efforts to speed up a scheduled increase in the minimum wage (from the current level of $1.25 to $1.60 in February 1967), the *Times* editors noted that because of the escalating rate of inflation (the consumer price index rose by 1.6 percent in 1965 and by 2.9 percent in 1966), "the pinch of higher living costs cuts most cruelly into the depressed budgets of workers in the lowest income brackets." They suggested that in the process of fighting inflation, the country's policy "cannot be conducted by condemning them [low-wage workers] to a steady erosion of purchasing power" and that the proposed pay increase would make it "a little easier for millions of such workers to bring up their families in some measure of decency" (Sept. 2, 1966). The editors made no mention of the possibility that the pay increase would backfire and cause unemployment and economic hardship for some minimum-wage workers.

Later that same month, the editors returned to the proposed minimum-wage increase that supposedly would help an estimated 4 million workers. This time they focused their attention on a different argument, however—namely, that the increase could be expected to have what might be called "trickle up" effects: "The impact of the higher standards will not be limited to those at the very bottom of the wage ladder. Other workers receiving wages 15, 25, or even 50 cents above the minimum will benefit by pushing up the bottom" (Sept. 17, 1966). However, the editors never attempted to explain how the higher-wage workers might benefit.[2] Although the editors complimented the union movement for its historical support of minimum-wage bills, they neglected saying that the increase would supplant lower-pay workers with fewer making more pay.

The editors paused only to assert that one of the nation's pressing needs "is for a program that will create more job opportunities for the unskilled and undereducated—the big unabsorbed lump among the unemployed"—and to suggest that creating a "social wage" designed to place a floor under family income might be more socially beneficial than further increases in the statutory minimum. In spite of the editors' interest in having the family income floor "unrelated to the performance of work," they insisted that the formula must contain adequate incentive for individual self-help, as against perpetual dependence (Sept. 17, 1966). Finally, with a higher federal minimum wage likely, the editors reversed their earlier position on the proposed $1.50 New York state minimum wage, saying that the discrepancy (between the state and federal minimums) was slight and the period when the state's minimum would be above that of the nation's minimum would be relatively brief (May 26, 1966).

The *Times* editors apparently were not impressed—at least, not publicly—by the sharply contrasting position taken by the *Wall Street*

FIGURE 4.1 Civilian unemployment rates for black and white male teenagers, 1954 to 1992

Percent

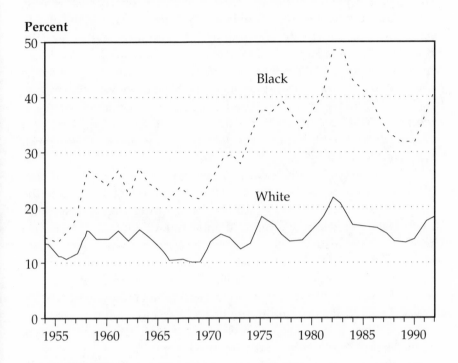

Note: Black covers black and other nonwhite male teenagers 1954–1972 and only black teenagers 1973–1992.

Source: *Economic Report of the President, 1993.*

Journal editors in July 1966.[3] The *Journal* editors claimed, citing a recent pamphlet written by University of Chicago economists Yale Brozen and Milton Friedman, that the minimum wage disproportionately increased the unemployment of black teenagers. As Figure 4.1 reveals, the civilian unemployment rates for all male teenagers, both black and white, were relatively high in 1954 (the first year for which data are available), 13.4 and 14.4 percent, respectively, and more than double the unemployment rate of all civilian workers. Still, the unemployment rates of black and white male teenagers were relatively close, separated by only a percentage point.[4] By 1965, however, the rates for black and white male teenagers had diverged significantly, not because the white male unemployment rate had grown (it remained at about 13 percent), but because the unemployment rate of black male teenagers had increased to 23.3 percent—up 60 percent.[5] It was this type of data that caused Brozen and Friedman to conclude that the minimum wage was one of the country's most racist laws, albeit unintentionally.[6] "Amid all the fanfare for new laws to help Negroes," the *Journal* editors wrote in a lead editorial, "it's especially ironic to see Congress so close to passing a measure [an increase in the minimum wage to $1.60 an hour] that would hurt them more than anyone else."[7] Without seeking to dispute such widely reported statistical claims, the *Times* editors continued to press for coverage of 5.6 million additional workers. Their chief concern remained farmworkers, who were, as a consequence of not being covered, the "most exploited of all American workers" (Mar. 14, 1966).

Nonetheless, unemployment rates among teenagers, especially black teenagers, continued to grow, as is evident in Figure 4.1 (until the early 1980s). Indeed, later in 1968, Professor Brozen argued that minimum-wage hikes were increasing the unemployment rate of teenagers relative to that of adults. He noted that the teenage unemployment rate shortly before the $1.15 minimum went into effect in September 1961 was 2.5 times the unemployment rate of the "total work-seeking population."[8] After the 1961 increase, the teenage unemployment rate increased to 2.7 times the adult rate in 1962, and to 3.4 times the adult rate after the increase to $1.25 in September 1963.[9] By the mid-1960s, even Arthur Burns, who had supported a minimum-wage increase while chairman of President Eisenhower's Council of Economic Advisors, changed his tune, making much the same point as had Brozen but arguing that "the ratio of the unemployment rate of teenagers to that of male adults was invariably higher during the six months following an increase in the minimum wage than it was in the preceding half year."[10] Such facts would, in the 1970s, come back to haunt the *Times* editors, first causing them to search for legislative means of moderating the detrimental effects of minimum-wage increases and, eventually, to reverse themselves once again.[11]

In February 1969, the *Times* editors noted that the Liberal Party in New York state wanted the state to become the first to guarantee a job to every person willing and able to work and to raise the state's minimum wage from the then $1.60 an hour to $2.50 an hour. They extolled party leaders for their "noble goals" and admonished the liberals to "bring forward new ideas, some of which may ultimately triumph." However, the editors returned to the arguments they had used earlier in opposition to a city-based minimum wage that would have been significantly higher and superseded the state and federal minimum wage. They concluded that a unilateral move by the state to raise the minimum wage was simply not "feasible": "New York State, rich and powerful as it is, is still only one of fifty states competing for shares in the national income. If it gets too far out ahead of the rest of the country, it will simply drive business and industry into other states" (Feb. 1, 1969).

In October 1969, in spite of the fact that the federal minimum wage had declined in real terms by 6 percent since its real-dollar peak the year before, the *Times* editors continued to pull back from their earlier unabashed support of minimum-wage increases. They took exception to a just proposed New York City Council ordinance that would require any city supplier to pay all of its workers at least $2.50 an hour (a rate 56 percent above the then federal minimum wage). The ordinance's supporters believed its passage would make the city a "pacesetter" for the nation. The editors suggested that the council was acting like King Canute, who, according to legend, had ordered that the tides be changed just to show his subjects that he did not have divine powers. However, the editors worried that council members were taking their authority more seriously and asked, "Is the city really going to check the wages of every company that sells gasoline, coffee, light bulbs, pillow cases and a million and one other commodities?" (Oct. 13, 1969).

More important, without expressing any sympathy whatsoever for low-wage workers, the editors denounced the proposal because "such an excessive minimum wage actually tends to hurt those the council members seek to help: the unskilled, the handicapped, the young. There are many such people whose services are simply not worth $2.50 an hour." Furthermore, they said, the council must understand that New York City is in competition with many other low-wage areas of the country, "so any effort really to enforce a $2.50 minimum would increase pressures for business to leave the city" (Oct. 13, 1969). They concluded by asking then Mayor Lindsay to veto the bill.

Another adjustment in the *Times* editors' position was evidenced when they supported Governor Rockefeller's proposal to increase the state's minimum wage from $1.60 to $1.85 an hour. Apparently, the editors felt the more modest increase of 16 percent was reasonable. They acknowledged that there was "some validity" to industrialists' arguments that the state's minimum wage, which with the increase would be above the federal minimum, would "put New York businesses at a cost disadvantage with competitors in other states." However, such considerations were outweighed, in this case, "by the unfairness—even unrealism—of expecting workers to take jobs at wages that bring them less income than they could get by doing nothing on relief." A minimum wage of $1.85 an hour would yield about $3,700 a year, slightly less than could be drawn by the average family of four on public relief. They concluded, "New York State cannot be an economic island, but it must establish stronger underpinnings for the economic welfare of those eager to be self-reliant" (Jan. 7, 1970).

The "Sensible Minimum" as a Shift toward the "Social Wage"

The *Times* editors had by 1971 repeatedly editorialized about the disastrous state of the nation's welfare system, arguing that a greater share of welfare payments should be covered by the federal government, because people from rural areas were migrating to urban areas where welfare benefits were more generous. In April 1971, the editors endorsed President Nixon's proposed reform of welfare and a proposal by Wilbur Mills, then chairman of the House Ways and Means Committee, to tie an increase in the federal minimum wage to $2 an hour to welfare reform. In Mills's view, the proposed tie-in would save federal welfare dollars. In the view of the editors, the tie-in would institutionalize their favored concept of a "social wage—one in which family need becomes a specific determinant in government wage regulation" (Apr. 26, 1971).

Once again, the editors acknowledged some of the most likely objections to the proposed 25 percent increase in the minimum wage: It would contribute to inflation and damage the employment opportunities of workers with "minimal skills, thus accentuating the very welfare problem Mr. Mills is seeking to abate." Such prospects, the editors reasoned, required "social inventiveness" in the formulation of welfare policy, at which point they recommended an early version of the wage subsidy that had long been on the *Times'* social agenda: "a program under which disadvantaged workers could be hired by employers, with the understanding that the community would pay, as a sort of training subsidy, part of the money they would otherwise get in welfare," a move that would give low-wage workers more job opportunities and higher pay (Apr. 26, 1971).

A year later in 1972, the editors again returned to the theme of the need for a "social wage" when Congress was reconsidering increasing, in two steps, the federal minimum wage to $2 an hour in 1974, which the editors tagged as the "sensible minimum." At the same time, they rejected the proposed minimum then before the Senate Labor Committee of $2.20

an hour and the "'must work' welfare abomination" before the Senate Finance Committee that would require welfare recipients to accept work for as little as $1.20 an hour (when the existing minimum wage was set at $1.60). They also commended the House for dropping a proposal that would have required the imposed compensatory tariffs and quotas on imports from countries whose wages were below the federal minimum wage. "The sole effect of the proposal would have been to stir retaliatory moves by other nations, reducing employment opportunities in this country instead of increasing them" (May 12, 1972).

Continuing their political balancing act, the *Times* editors opposed a new Senate bill in mid-1972 that would raise the minimum wage to $2 immediately and to $2.20 the following year, and they suggested that the "House was on sounder grounds in voting a twenty-cent increase now and another twenty cents next year" (June 24, 1972). It appears that the editors were unwilling to go along with the Senate bill because they wanted to couple a more modest wage floor increase with an expansion of the coverage of the minimum-wage law. The Senate Labor and Public Works Committee had just recommended that the federal minimum wage be made applicable for the first time to the 5 million federal, state, and local government workers, 2 million retail workers, and 1 million domestic workers, and that the 30-cent gap between the federal minimum and the special agriculture minimum be gradually eliminated over several years. The editors endorsed the extended coverage without, again, explicitly indicating they were aware of the potential detrimental employment effects. At the same time, they appeared to be groping for an acceptable level of increase in unemployment among covered workers that, presumably, would define a "sensible" minimum wage.

"Marie Antoinette seems to have taken over as dictator of policy on Capitol Hill," charged the *Times* editors in the fall of 1972. At their rhetorical best, they avoided mentioning the deleterious effects of unemployment from minimum-wage increases they had acknowledged in earlier editorials. They condemned Congress and the Nixon administration for failing to reach a compromise on the minimum wage, thus "slamming the door on the nation's poorest citizens, both those on welfare and those working for sweatshop wages." They fretted that the actions of the "feuding factions" in Congress provided little "optimism that decency would prevail," which, in the minds of the editors, would require that the minimum wage be raised in two steps to $2.20 an hour and that coverage be extended—in other words, the outcome would resemble the House proposals the *Times* had backed from the start (Oct. 5, 1972).

Flirtation with the Subminimum Wage
and the Search for a "Workable Compromise"

Following the defeat of all minimum-wage increase proposals in 1972, supporters of an even higher minimum pressed for another bill in 1973 and found support in the Nixon administration. The *Times* editors also supported the proposal, which included an increase from $1.60 to $1.90 an hour, with a lower "hiring-in" wage floor for teenagers. While still looking for a "sensible floor" that would not destroy job opportunities for teenagers "whose unemployment is roughly four times that for older workers," they also had other concerns. One was that any immediate wage increase that reestablished the purchasing power of the minimum wage when it was last adjusted upward, five years before, "would have ripple effects in other wages that would help feed the already disturbing inflationary tide" (Apr. 11, 1973). The editors complained, once again, that the proposal did not extend coverage.

Nevertheless, they acknowledged in late summer 1973 that President Nixon might veto a minimum-wage bill requiring a $2 floor, if the bill failed to include a special subminimum wage for teenagers "whose unemployment rates were inordinately high" (Aug. 5, 1973). The editors admitted that a subminimum would be desirable to preserve teenage employment. "But," they concluded, "the hardship that would be inflicted by denying a general increase in the minimum to millions of the working poor and by preventing the extension of coverage to eight million now excluded workers . . . would be incalculably greater than any possible damage the law might do in drying up new job openings" (Aug. 28, 1973).

Such arguments, however, failed to impress the unions that, the *Times* editors thought, had "dug in so intractably against a lower minimum for youth" or President Nixon, who shortly after the latest *Times* editorial carried out his threat by vetoing the minimum-wage bill. Again, while simultaneously acknowledging the president's legitimate concern for teenage employment and ignoring the fact that not all minimum-wage workers live in poverty, the editors declared that the existing disagreement between the administration and the union movement "cannot be allowed to stand forever as an obstacle to extending economic justice to millions of low-income workers whose families are slowly starving as inflation bleeds their slender earnings" (Sept. 7, 1973). What was needed was a "workable compromise."

Only two weeks later, the failure of the House to override the president's veto prompted the editors to wax eloquent once again about the cruelty innate in failing to reach a compromise. They called the

44

administration's concern over teenage joblessness an "arguable proposition" and chided both sides for relying on "dubious slogans and statistics." Millions of low-income workers—especially farm laborers, "still the most abused group in the national work force—cannot be permanently held ransom while the warring groups on Capitol Hill posture over the special minimum wage for youths on the periphery of the job market" (Sept. 20, 1973). Since inflation during the previous six months had broached an annual rate of 10 percent (which the *Times* editors attributed to the relaxation of Phase II of the Nixon price-control system) (Dec. 23, 1973), the minimum wage would have to be adjusted in the fall of 1973 to $2.12 (merely to reestablish purchasing power parity with the peak value of the minimum wage in 1968) (Sept. 22, 1973). Even then, low-wage workers could expect to see their purchasing power fall with the inflation rate of 10 percent projected by the administration for the next year (Oct. 6, 1973).

By late 1973, the authority of what some were calling the "Imperial Presidency" had been weakened greatly by the emerging Watergate scandal coupled with the energy crisis and double-digit inflation. These, the editors wrote, "had devastated Mr. Nixon's once-impregnable [political] position." Much to the astonishment of the editors, Congress in November 1973, in response to his "brutal bombing" of Cambodia, overrode President Nixon's veto of the War Powers Act (Dec. 23, 1973). The juxtaposition of the Nixon administration's political problems, along with additional calls for reconsideration of a minimum-wage increase, indicated that the *Times* felt the time was at hand for its long-sought and now "desperately needed" so-called "sensible compromise" (in the name of poor workers afflicted with more than five years of inflation without a single adjustment in pay).

Now seeming to be more amenable to the Nixon position on the subminimum wage for teenagers, the editors at the *Times* suggested that unions were being unreasonably obstinate on the issue (Feb. 9, 1974). However, as the purchasing power of the minimum wage continued to erode, the editors rapidly shifted in 1973 from implied acceptance of the subminimum (with repeated mention of teenage employment problems) to outright objection to it as "hardly significant enough to become the controlling element in determining whether the President once again vetoes a minimum-wage bill needed to rescue millions of families from privation" (with no mention of teenage employment problems) (Mar. 2, 1974). After all, the existing $2 minimum had lost more than 38 percent of its purchasing power between 1968 and late March 1974 (Mar. 2, 24, 1974).

With the impeachment drumbeat being heard throughout Congress and the White House, President Nixon, perhaps encouraged by *Times* editorials, caved in and signed a compromise minimum-wage bill in April 1974, one that raised the minimum to $2 an hour in June, to $2.10 on January 1, 1975, and to $2.30 on January 1, 1976, and that extended coverage to 7 million federal, state, and local government workers. Aside from stressing that minimum-wage workers would still remain below the 1968 parity level, the editors complained that the long delay in the adjustment meant that the immediate 25 percent increase would have an unfortunate inflationary "ripple effect" on the pay of higher-paid workers: "Differentials between various skill levels are difficult to tamper with. In jobs where the statutory pay floor tends also to be the ceiling, freezing that floor too long in a period of rampant inflation is not only unjust but also unstabilizing" (Apr. 12, 1974).

With three increases in the minimum wage already scheduled, the editors at the *Times* did not feel compelled to address the minimum wage issue again until February 1976. By then, their tune had changed significantly, very likely in part because the economy had gone through a recession. At the time, the overall unemployment rate was 7.8 percent, while for blacks and other minorities it was 13.2 percent and, for teenagers, 19.9 percent—facts on which the editors based an editorial that called for "modifying the minimum-wage laws to avoid shutting low-skilled young people out of jobs." The editors did not say, however, how the minimum-wage laws should be modified; they merely added that Congress should consider the development of public service jobs and add "wage subsidies to private employers" (Feb. 7, 1976).

Notes

1. Here the editors recognized that economic development groups from other areas of the country would use New York's municipal minimum wage in their campaigns to attract businesses out of the city.
2. Given later editorials, I can only imagine that the editors were thinking of wage differentials that tend to be maintained between skill levels.
3. "An Anti-Negro Law," *Wall Street Journal*, July 13, 1966 (editorial), p. 14.
4. The unemployment rate of black female teenagers in 1954 (20.6 percent) was substantially higher than the unemployment rate for white female teenagers (10.4 percent).
5. The unemployment rate of white female teenagers grew from 10.6 to 14 percent, but the unemployment rate of black female teenagers grew from 20.6 to 31.7 percent.
6. Friedman repeated his argument that the minimum wage would adversely affect the employment opportunities of women, teenagers, and minorities (especially black teenagers) in his regular column for *Newsweek* ("Minimum Wage Rates," [Sept. 26, 1966], as reprinted in Milton Friedman, *An Economist's Protest: Columns in Political Economy* [Glen Ridge, NJ: Thomas Harden, 1972], pp. 144–145).
7. The *Journal* editors led off their editorial with what must have been to them a very pleasing quotation from Professor Friedman: "Of all the laws on the statute books of this country, I believe the minimum-wage law probably does the Negroes the most harm. It is not intended to be an anti-Negro law but, in fact, it is" (as quoted in "An Anti-Negro Law," *Wall Street Journal*, July 13, 1966 [editorial], p. 14).
8. As reported in "How to Keep Teenagers Idle," *Wall Street Journal*, Oct. 18, 1968 (editorial), p. 16.
9. Ibid. The teenage unemployment rate rose to 3.6 times the adult rate in 1968, the year in which the real minimum wage peaked. Teenage relative unemployment generally fell through the 1970s and 1980s along with the real minimum wage. In 1987, the teenage unemployment rate was down to 2.6 times the adult rate (author's calculations).
10. As quoted in "Minimum Wages and Minimum Jobs," *Wall Street Journal*, June 4, 1971 (editorial), p. 6.
11. Actually, later econometric work done on the impact of minimum-wage increases on the employment of black and white teenagers leaves at least some room for disputing the claim that the minimum-wage law was, albeit unintentionally, racist in its effect.

    As suggested by the claim that the law may in its effect be "racist," a majority of the studies reviewed by Charles Brown, Curtis Gilroy, and Andrew Cohen found that the elasticity of demand for black teenagers was higher than that for white teenagers. However, several studies found the exact opposite, or that the minimum-wage increases studied may have increased the unemployment rates of teenage whites more than that of blacks (see Brown, Gilroy, and Cohen, "The Effects of the

Minimum Wage on Employment and Unemployment,," *Journal of Economic Literature* [June 1982], Table 3, p. 504).

CHAPTER 5

The Second About-Face

The most recent turnaround in the *Times* minimum-wage position occurred in March 1977 and was preceded by changes in several key journalistic positions at the paper. The switch was also heralded by what might be described—using scholarly, academic standards—as a virtual torrent of research on the economic consequences of past minimum-wage increases.

In 1977, Arthur Ochs Sulzberger remained as publisher, a spot he had held since 1963. However, A. M. Rosenthal had been promoted in 1976 from managing editor to executive editor. Long-time editorial-page head John B. Oats was moved to senior editor, and Max Frankel was moved from editor of the Sunday edition to manager of the editorial page (a position he held until 1987, at which point he was replaced by Jack Rosenthal). In addition, Seymour Topping, who had been Rosenthal's assistant, replaced Rosenthal as managing editor in 1976. Charlotte Curtis, Clifton Daniel, and Tom Wicker all remained as associate editors.

The Empirical Evidence

Perhaps the build-up of a substantial body of casual and econometric evidence on the employment effects of the minimum wage was just as important as the personnel changes. Almost all of this research showed that previous minimum-wage increases had caused statistically significant job losses, especially for teenagers (for whom a 10 percent increase in the minimum might reduce employment by 1 to 3 percent).[1] Although the computed effects were weaker (generally, less than 1 percent job loss for each 10 percent increase in the minimum), research was also showing reductions in employment opportunities for adults 20 to 24 years old and for elderly males.[2]

Overall, the stock of major articles on the minimum wage in print almost tripled in the decade prior to 1977, though many studies were not

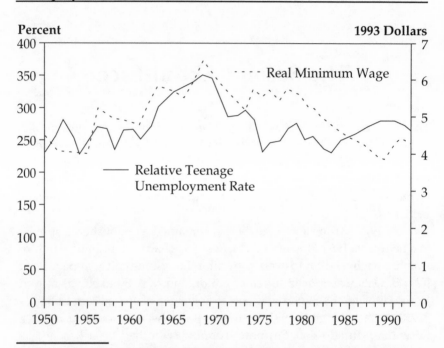

Source: *Economic Report of the President, 1993;* and author's calculations.

published in top academic journals and collected works. One such non-journal study found that the 1972 increase in the minimum wage had resulted in an annual loss of approximately 320,000 jobs for teenagers and that if there had been no minimum-wage law in 1976, the teenage unemployment rate would have been 3.8 percentage points lower.[3] The subsequent growth in minimum-wage articles after 1977 indicates that much additional, unpublished research was available in 1977.[4]

However, by the late 1970s, an editor did not have to be an econometrician to deduce a strong link between the minimum wage and teenage unemployment. Figure 5.1 shows the remarkably close relationship that existed throughout the mid-1970s between the *real* minimum wage and the unemployment rate of teenagers relative to that of the total civilian unemployment rate. Note that the teenage unemployment rate peaked at 353 percent of the civilian unemployment rate in the same year that the real minimum wage reached its all-time peak of $6.58 an hour.[5] As can be

50

seen in Figure 5.1, the very close fit was obviously broken to a degree in the middle to late 1980s. Nevertheless, by the mid-1980s the causal relationship between increases in both the minimum wage and teenage unemployment had been firmly established in a number of econometric studies that the *Times* editors found convincing.

Economists' Views

Because evidence based on employment figures was mounting that job losses were at least partially attributable to minimum-wage increases and the evidence was supported by sophisticated econometric studies, economists, especially those who specialized in the emerging field of public choice economics, began to oppose further increases publicly and to investigate the issue of why "good economics" so often makes for "bad politics."[6] In its 1975 report, President Ford's Council of Economic Advisors, headed by Alan Greenspan, argued that the recent escalation of teenage unemployment could be attributed, in part, to the minimum wage, which had also resulted in a significant loss of on-the-job training for teenagers: "The youths who suffer most would be precisely those who might need the most help—youth with little schooling and greater difficulties and those subject to discrimination."[7] Andrew Brimmer, a Harvard economics professor who had been a governor of the Federal Reserve Board, publicly denounced the proposed increases and called for a reduction in the minimum wage as a means of increasing the employment chances of black teenagers.[8] Even President Carter's labor secretary, economics professor Ray Marshall, publicly conceded that the proposed increase in the minimum wage that he supported would cause "100,000 or so" American workers to lose their jobs.[9]

The eighth edition of Professor Paul Samuelson's principles of economics textbook reflected the tenor of the mounting evidence on minimum wages: "These [minimum-wage laws] often hurt those they are designed to help. What good does it do a black youth to know that an employer must pay him $1.60 per hour if the fact that he must be paid that amount is what keeps him from getting a job."[10] After surveying the available literature on the minimum wage in 1978, UCLA labor economist Finis Welch emphatically concluded:

> If there is a general theme to the empirical literature on the subject, it is that the simple theoretical predictions are confirmed. Almost every serious scholar of minimum wages

would argue (on the basis of available evidence) that minimum wages have reduced employment for those who would otherwise earn low wages, particularly teenagers.[11]

More generally, by the late 1970s, 90 percent of the 600 academic, business, and government economists surveyed agreed with the proposition that "a minimum wage increases unemployment among youth and unskilled workers."[12]

Nevertheless, union officials and many Democratic members of Congress pressed for further increases in the minimum. Because of the time and resources required to get the preceding minimum-wage bill passed, unions shifted ground and sought a minimum wage that, for the first time, would be indexed to average industrial wages and, therefore, would not require congressional action every few years. Chairman John Dent of the House's Labor Standards Subcommittee recommended that the then existing minimum wage of $2.30 be adjusted upward to 55 percent of the average hourly wage of production workers in 1977, which would mean a minimum wage of $2.85 ($6.77 in February 1993 prices), and to 60 percent of the average wage in 1978, which would mean a projected average wage of $3.30 ($7.24 in February 1993 prices).

The Editorial Shift

In their March 21, 1977, lead editorial, the *Times* editors noted in passing that the fortunes of the lowest wage earners would, if the new minimum wage were adopted, be tied to the "fortunes of industrial workers, eliminating the need for periodic Congressional amendments." Then, without any clue of what was coming, the *Times* editors must have stunned their former political allies when they wrote:

> Since the Depression, liberals have favored higher minimum wages while conservatives have resisted. But this debate has become sterile. *Whatever the merits of minimum wages in the past, they make little economic sense today, whether determined by indexing or in the old-fashioned way.*
>
> Organized labor favors a high minimum wage because that reduces management's resistance to union recruiting. Where cheap alternative sources of labor are eliminated, high-priced union labor no longer looks so bad to company managers. Support for a minimum wage floor also comes from people with generous hearts. Is it fair, they ask, to require anyone to

work for $70 or $80 a week, the take-home pay of employees
earning the $2.30 minimum? (emphasis added)

The editors went on to add that while the absence of a higher minimum
wage, may not be fair, it "offers no remedy" (a major theme of their
opposition ever since). They stressed that employers would respond to
the higher minimum by curtailing production and switching to labor-saving machinery, the result of which would be that the majority of the
workers covered by the proposed $2.85 minimum "would benefit by
higher paychecks. But some workers would be laid off or forced into the
fringe of the labor market not covered by the minimum-wage laws." They
acknowledged not knowing just how many workers would be unemployed, but that "rough calculations put the figure at between 200,000 and
one million" (Mar. 21, 1977).

The *Times* editors recognized that members of Congress from the
North saw a higher minimum-wage law as a means of stemming the flow
of industry to the South. They agreed that a higher minimum might make
northern cities more competitive with small towns in (they specifically
mentioned) Mississippi, but a hitch remained:

> Some poor people would benefit at the expense of other poor
> people. And if a higher minimum wage did shift more un-
> skilled jobs to the Snowbelt, would anyone up North really
> want the result—more unemployed people in Mississippi with
> no choice but to head for those jobs in Detroit?"

The editors made their about-face complete by rejecting the concept of the
subminimum for teenagers, calling it an idea that has a "certain appeal"
but noting a basic flaw: the subminimum would encourage the substitution of teenage workers for adult workers. The editors also cited the
"discovery" by University of Michigan economist and Brookings Institution scholar Edward Gramlich that many teenage minimum-wage workers were from middle-class families and were "not the intended
beneficiaries of the lower youth minimum." And they concluded, more
importantly, "A higher minimum wage is no answer to poverty, and the
indexing gimmick can't work any better to improve the lot of the neediest
citizens" (Mar. 21, 1977).

The editors returned to a frontal denunciation of the proposed
minimum-wage bill in August 1977, when they ran yet another lead
editorial with a headline that clearly announced their position: "The Cruel
Cost of the Minimum Wage." In this editorial, the first of a series with
gradually more sophisticated arguments, they implicitly relied on econo-

mists' favorite analytical tool, the law of demand: "A business hires workers only if their labor produces earnings at least equal to their wages. If the business is compelled to pay $2.65, it cannot hire those whose work produces less than that." They stressed that the proposed increase would "destroy the jobs at the very bottom," again citing statistics showing that the unemployment rate among teenagers was close to 20 percent and up to 40 percent among black teenagers. They once again attacked the proposed subminimum on the grounds that the law would discriminate in employment against adults and that "a 40-year-old textile worker with a family has just as much right to a job as a 17-year-old high school dropout." The editors once again cited the findings of Professor Gramlich, but this time they gave figures: "Fully 40 percent [of the poorly paid, unskilled teenage workers] live with families whose incomes exceed $15,000 per year" (or 11 percent above the median family income in 1977). They concluded that enactment of the proposed minimum-wage bill could merely "intensify the cruel competition among the poor for scarce jobs" (Aug. 17, 1977). In a rare tipping of their hat to competitors, the editors of the *Wall Street Journal* commended the *Times* editors for "cogently" explaining the minimum wages' faults to the *Times'* readers who might have remained "Doubting Thomases."[13]

The *Times* editors next concluded that the then more rapid pace of economic development in the South might be slowed by three bills already passed or in Congress: the Clean Air Act, the national energy plan, and the minimum-wage bill. They pointed out that the proposed minimum-wage bill would hit the South hardest simply because it has "more workers at the lowest wages."[14]

By the end of August, the editors returned to print with another editorial against the minimum wage (Aug. 29, 1977), spurred very likely by a rash of letters from outraged readers.[15] For the first time, the editors cited recent econometric research (without identifying the exact source) showing that with every 10 percent increase in the minimum wage, between 25,000 and 125,000 jobs for teenagers were eliminated. Then with a leap of statistical intuition, and no reported evidence, they suggested, "If the minimum wage has a similar impact on other unskilled workers— and there is every reason to believe it does—the effect on the total labor force must be three times as great" (Aug. 29, 1977). In response to an argument by Clarence Mitchell that the minimum wage does not destroy jobs[16] but rather prevents new jobs from being created, the editors replied, "We do not find this distinction reassuring." They agreed that it would be nice to live in a world in which everyone could "get one of those well-paying jobs," but stated, "The plain fact is that some unskilled workers aren't sufficiently productive to earn that much more" (Aug. 29, 1977).

When the House passed the minimum-wage bill in September 1977, the *Times* editors again assailed the scheduled three annual increases as an affront to employment opportunities of the least-skilled workers. In December, the editors went on the offensive, acknowledging that nothing could be done at that point to stop the increase in the minimum wage from $2.65 to $2.90 but asking that Congress consider freezing the minimum to reduce the employment and inflation damage done. If a freeze could not be obtained, then the scheduled increases should be postponed or scaled back. Again, they cited the work of Gramlich, who had found that employers must pay an additional dollar to other, higher-paid workers for every additional dollar paid to minimum-wage workers. The editors argued that if nothing else could be done, Congress should consider the "two-track" minimum wage. Given the upward spiraling inflation rate at the time, the editors conceded that "the chance that some adult jobs will be lost seems worth taking" (Sept. 20, 1977).

In 1980, the editors cautiously endorsed then presidential candidate Reagan's proposal to create a subminimum wage for teenagers, reasoning that while a "two-tier" wage system was probably flawed (it might create some new jobs but it might also give employers an incentive to substitute teenagers for adult workers), they agreed that "it is probably worth a try." They reasoned again that the proposed minimum-wage hike might raise the amount of income that goes to the 5 percent of the labor force covered by the minimum, but they also noted that economists (who went unnamed) had determined that "every 10 percent increase in the minimum reduces jobs available to the unskilled by about 7 percent." Moreover, the editors reiterated a point made earlier: Many of the minimum-wage jobs would go to the "children of the middle class, displacing poor adults," making the minimum wage a "poor substitute for direct Government aid to the working poor." Toward the end of the year, they suggested for the first time that while abolition of the minimum wage was not in the political "cards" (because of union opposition), the "best course would be to abandon the minimum wage altogether and to use tax credits and even wage subsidies to help the lowest-paid workers toward a better life" (Dec. 2, 1980).

The *Times* editors did not return with a full editorial on the minimum wage for the next two years, but when they did, they renewed their call for guarded consideration of the subminimum equal to 85 percent of the minimum wage, because of the persistent high unemployment among teenagers.[17] But in March 1983, at the same time that they were raising doubts about the worth of various multibillion-dollar jobs bills that were floating around Congress (since "public works projects deliver relatively small bang for the buck; they are expensive and slow to develop"), the editors seemed to backtrack somewhat on the subminimum (possibly because the employment picture was improving). They concluded that the proposed subminimum and tax credit for hiring teenage workers might "tempt employers to hire a less expensive worker in place of one already employed, for no net jobs gain" (Mar. 14, 1983). Nevertheless, later in the month the editors again concluded that the Reagan administration's proposed three-year "experiment" with a subminimum for workers under 20 years old (with no increase in the adult minimum) should be adopted. If appropriately structured, the proposed experiment would answer the question that had been stalling the debate: "Would employers simply replace older workers with eligible youth?" (Mar. 21, 1985).[18] Indeed, the editors were willing to go along with the administration on other free-market-oriented policy proposals. For example, they did not see the Reagan administration's proposal to allow industrial work at home (specifically, knitwear) as a threat to the minimum wage; they proposed that homework be encouraged, especially given the growth in computer technology that advanced telecommunications.[19] Moreover, the editors endorsed Reagan's proposed experiment with "enterprise zones" (in which, according to early versions of the proposal, employers might not have to pay the minimum wage or abide by a host of other federal, state, and local regulations) (Feb. 11, 1985).

Proposed Abolition

Although openly hostile to proposed minimum-wage increases in 1986, the editors continued to print letters and columns hostile to their editorial position. By 1986, however, even the proponents of minimum-wage increases were admitting that increases would eliminate jobs. Two proponents acknowledged that the Federal Minimum Wage Study Commission, appointed by President Carter, found that a 10 percent increase in the minimum wage would decrease "teen-age employment by 1 percent" (one-seventh the impact the editors had reported in 1980).[20]

The *Times* editors were obviously unimpressed by the statistical claims of minimal damage from minimum-wage increases made by proponents and printed on their op-ed page. In January 1987, they capped their about-face on the minimum wage with a call for its total elimination. As they had done many times since 1977, they sympathized with "some liberals" who continued to back minimum-wage increases, saying that "the working poor obviously deserve a better shake." Nonetheless, they insisted there were "catches" to the proposed increases. They would raise unemployment among the most unfortunate workers:

> A higher minimum would undoubtedly raise the living standard of the majority of low-wage workers who could keep their jobs. That again, it is argued, would justify the sacrifice of the minority who became unemployable. The argument isn't convincing. Those at the greatest risk from a higher minimum would be the young, poor workers, who already face formidable barriers to getting and keeping jobs. Indeed, President Reagan has proposed a *lower* minimum wage just to improve their chances of finding work.

Instead, the editors recommended the provision of training and education programs and "wage supplements" for low-income workers. They acknowledged that only "mixed results" had been obtained from the "dozens of programs" to improve the labor market skills of low-income workers; however, "The concept isn't necessarily at fault; nurturing the potential of individuals raised in poverty is very difficult. A humane society would learn from its mistakes and keep on trying." The "wage supplements" could come in the form of cash; payments for medical insurance, pensions, and Social Security; additional earned-income tax credits; or a "negative income tax" paying up to $800 per year to poor families (Jan. 14, 1987).

As if they were seeking to regain the confidence of their liberal readers and admirers, the *Times* editors returned to print a month after they called for the abolition of the minimum wage with a lead editorial entitled "Look: Liberalism!" They noted that new forms of liberalism, with which they obviously wanted to be identified, were again springing up "everywhere like daffodils through the melting snows of the Reagan revolution." This time around, stunned by the stigma of the "L-word," liberals were not only renaming themselves (going by "progressives" and "neo-liberals"), they were beginning to rethink their favored programs and to propose new ways of accomplishing their old objective of helping the poor in ways that would "no longer be wishful or wasteful." They noted—perhaps referring to themselves as much as anyone else (although they specifically identified Senator Edward Kennedy and Senator Patrick Moynihan)—that "soft hearts have grown hard noses. It's a doubly welcome combination, one that might win broad support and help rescue poverty's next generation."[27]

The debate over the minimum wage was probably never in a greater log jam than in the three years following the January 1987 *Times* editorial. Shortly after the editorial ran, Senator Kennedy introduced his minimum-wage bill that, if enacted, would have raised the minimum wage in three steps to $4.65 on January 1, 1990. Thereafter, the minimum wage would be adjusted annually to equal 50 percent of the "average private, nonsupervisory, nonagricultural hourly wage" (rounded to the nearest multiple of 5 cents).[22] Fifty-four economists—including Nobel laureate Lawrence Klein, retired Harvard Professor John Kenneth Galbraith, and MIT's Sloan Business School Dean Lester Thurow—signed an open letter of support for the minimum wage: "The evidence sharply refutes arguments [that minimum-wage increases cause unemployment]. Six times this nation has raised the minimum wage and the historical evidence offers no evidence of significant employment and business disruption"[23] This widely reprinted statement drew an immediate condemnation, printed on the *Times* editorial page by Hoover Institution economist John Raisian and University of Chicago economist George Stigler.[24]

Both the democratic-controlled Congress and the republican Reagan administration dug in, ready to hold their ground on what quickly became an ideological impasse for both President Reagan and Senator Kennedy, among others, and a largely empirical debate over how many jobs would be lost. The contrast in the statistical argument was never sharper than in commentaries by American Enterprise Institute economist Marvin Kosters and the cochairman of the Citizen's Committee for a Just Minimum Wage, Arthur Flemming. Kosters argued in his *Wall Street Journal* column that, when the expanded coverage is considered, the actual "effective (average) wage" of minimum-wage workers was higher in 1987 than in the 1950s and 1960s.[25] In contrast, Flemming maintained in his letter to the editor of the *New York Times* that the Wharton macroeconometric model predicted adoption of the proposed 1987 increase would result in a tenth of a percent increase in total U.S. employment.[26] However, opponents touted (and most of the supporters acknowledged) that the Kennedy bill would eliminate at least 100,000 jobs, a fact aired by the *Times* editors in another opposing editorial after the Kennedy bill was introduced (Apr. 15, 1987).

Until his tenure in office was over in 1989, President Reagan stood staunchly against any increase in the minimum wage and kept his threat to veto an increase on the table. Senator Kennedy, however, remained adamant throughout 1988 in seeking a substantial increase (38 percent by 1990) and a legislated tie-in between the minimum wage and the average wage of production workers. That year, the *Times* editors no doubt fueled the debate by continuing to side with the opponents. In a series of five follow-up editorials run in 1988 and 1989, the editors accepted the Kennedy contention that the "minimum wage is not a subsistence wage . . . and does not permit full-time workers to provide the bare necessities for their families,"[27] but they pressed the issue that hundreds of thousands of jobs would be lost if the Kennedy proposal were ever enacted, citing as their authority the Department of Labor. The editors repeatedly asked that less counterproductive measures be found to help low-wage workers: "Raising the minimum wage is not cost free, just cost-concealing. Congress owes the working poor well-designed help, not a well-intentioned illusion" (Feb. 23, 1988). They continued to press for wage subsidies or income-tax credits for low-income workers into 1989, calling for, on more than one occasion, a veto of any new minimum-wage bill on the grounds that a veto would "clear the decks for a fresh bipartisan look at the earned income tax credit."[28]

When the editors and everyone else realized that a new minimum-wage bill would soon be passed and signed by President Bush, they became less quarrelsome about having a zero minimum wage and endorsed, somewhat reluctantly, the political compromise that the Bush administration and Congress had struck: a minimum wage of $4.25 an hour had to be coupled with an increase in tax credits for the working poor. The editors complimented the president for "rightly" preferring tax credits to a higher minimum wage, because "most low-wage workers, like students, are not from poor families. . . . The number of lost jobs may not be large but many of them would have gone to the cost disadvantaged youths." Rather than actually supporting the compromise, the editors appeared to accept the compromise as a matter of political expediency, reasoning that conceding to the higher minimum was probably the only way to get the $5 billion in additional tax credits for the truly disadvantaged workers. They also suggested that the higher minimum might reduce the cost, measured by lost revenues, of the tax credits (Nov. 2, 1989).

The *Times* capped its 1989 editorial campaign on the minimum wage with one last shot at what it now saw as the "regrettable subminimum 'training wage'" for teenagers (which in the early 1970s it had sought): "That [training wage] provides a needless incentive to substitute teenagers for older workers" (Nov. 2, 1989).

In the very early 1990s, the editors at the *Times* were joined in their opposition to municipal minimum wages by the editors at the *Washington Post*. The District of Columbia's Wage and Hour Board proposed to raise the district's minimum to $7.25 an hour, $3 above the federal minimum, only to compromise on a $5.25 wage. The *Post* editors tagged the original district proposal as the "killer minimum," stressing in a series of editorials a point that their counterparts at the *Times* had made many years before: The city was not an economic island, and the minimum wage, coupled with a host of other costly labor laws, was causing many jobs to move to the suburbs in Virginia and Maryland.[29] Of course, the editors at the *Wall Street Journal* continued their unbroken record of open hostility to any and every minimum-wage proposal, to the hypocrisy of top cabinet officers in the Bush administration who maintained that the 1989 minimum-wage law would cost "only" 200,000 jobs,[30] and to members of Congress who continued to maintain that they should not be covered by minimum-wage (or any other labor) laws.[31] The *Journal* editors also continued to give prominent exposure to the views of columnists that the teenage employment rate soared in the 1980s when the minimum wage was held at $3.35 an hour, only to fall almost as dramatically when it was once again raised in 1990 and 1991, points that have been at the heart of the *Times* editors' opposition.[32]

In 1992, a debate on the minimum wage reemerged among economists. For the first time in years, several economists had found evidence that the minimum wage may not adversely affect employment. In 1993, one of them, Lawrence Katz, was appointed chief economist under Secretary of Labor Robert Reich, known to be a supporter of raising the minimum wage. However, these new studies were soon challenged for having defective methodologies.[33]

In early 1993, the newly installed Clinton administration served notice that it intended to press for another round of increases in the minimum wage, starting with, perhaps, raising the minimum wage from $4.25 to above $5 an hour and then tying the minimum wage to the average wage of production workers from then on. However, later that year Clinton officials served notice that they intended to delay consideration of a much smaller increase (possibly to $4.50 or $4.75 an hour) until 1994, mainly because the economy was too weak for another hike in the minimum wage.[34]

Until June 1993, the *Times* remained remarkably quiet on the new federal minimum-wage debate, just as it had not commented on New Jersey's 1992 state minimum-wage increase to $5.20.[35] However, in June, the editors may have begun, albeit tentatively, to shift their position again. Concerned that the Clinton administration might sacrifice the needs of the poor in its efforts to reduce the deficit through a cutback in its proposed higher earned-income tax credit, a cutback the *Times* argued would be "an unconscionable blow to the needy," the editors suggested that the "wisest way to combat that erosion [in the real-dollar value of the minimum wage since 1991] is to combine tax credits with a slightly higher minimum wage that would be indexed to offset inflation."[36]

Whether this brief statement represents another turnaround is unclear. The editorial was obviously not intended to be a full-fledged discussion of the minimum wage; the earned-income tax credit, which the *Times* editors had supported for years, was the central concern. The editors were not asking for an increase in the *real* minimum, and they seemed to be concerned that any reduction in the proposed earned-income tax credit would necessarily lead to a higher minimum wage than otherwise—and to a level that is higher than would be reasonable. Nevertheless, the editors comments suggest that they may no longer be holding firmly to their previous goal of a zero minimum wage.

Notes

1. The most important of these and later minimum-wage articles are reviewed in Charles Brown, Curtis Gilroy, and Andrew Cohen, "The Effect of the Minimum Wage on Employment and Unemployment," *Journal of Economic Literature*, (June 1982), pp. 487–528. These authors and the Minimum Wage Study Commission shared the conclusion that the demand for teenage labor had an elasticity coefficient of .1 to .3 (ibid., and U.S. Department of Labor, *Report of the Minimum Wage Study Commission*, vol. 1 [Washington, DC: U.S. Government Printing Office, 1981]). However, it should be stressed that the minimum wage remained the subject of scholarly debate because not all studies showed negative effects. Indeed, several studies found a positive impact of minimum-wage increases on the unemployment rates (as distinguished from employment rates) of specified groups of workers. See Thomas G. Moore, "The Effects of Minimum Wages on Teenage Unemployment Rates," *Journal of Political Economy*, (July–Aug. 1971), pp. 897–903; and Douglas K. Adie, "The Lag Effects of Minimum Wages on Teenage Unemployment," *Proceedings of the Industrial Relations Research Association*, 24th annual meeting, New Orleans (Dec. 27–28, 1971), pp. 38–46.

2. This conclusion is supported by Jacob Mincer, "Unemployment Effects of Minimum Wages," *Journal of Political Economy*, (Aug. 1976, part 2), pp. S87–S105. However, Edward Gramlich found that the minimum wage caused a statistically insignificant reduction on the employment of adult males and had no impact on the employment of adult females (Gramlich, "Impact of Minimum Wages, Employment and Family Incomes," *Brookings Papers* [Washington, DC: Brookings Institution, 1976], pp. 261–268). See also Brown, Gilroy, and Cohen, "The Effect of the Minimum Wage on Employment and Unemployment," Table 6, p. 513.

3. James F. Ragan, Jr., *Minimum Wage Legislation and the Youth Labor Market* (St. Louis: Center for the Study of American Business, Washington University, 1976).

4. The number of major articles on the minimum wage totaled 43 in 1967 and 105 by the end of 1976. An additional 32 articles were printed in the 1977–1980 period (author's count as reported in the *Index of Economic Articles*). The onslaught of journal articles on the minimum wage was so great in the ensuing years that Mary Eccles and Richard Freeman felt compelled to title their minimum wage article, "What! Another Minimum Wage Study?" (*American Economic Review* [May 1982], pp. 226–232).

5. A plotting of the unemployment rate for black teenage males relative to the real minimum wage follows much the same pattern as in Figure 5.1.

6. F. G. Stendle, "The Appeal of Minimum Wage Laws and the Invisible Hand in Government," *Public Choice* (Spring 1973), pp. 133–136; William R. Keech, "More on the Vote Winning and Vote Losing Qualities of Minimum Wage Laws," *Public Choice* (Spring 1977), pp. 133–137; and Keith B. Leffler, "Minimum Wages, Welfare, and Wealth Transfers," *Journal of Law and Economics* (Oct. 1978), pp. 345–358.

7. Executive Office of the President, Council of Economic Advisors, *Economic Report of the President, 1975* (Washington, DC: U.S. Government Printing Office, 1975), p. 107. William Fellner and Gary Seevers were the other two members of the council.

8. As reported in "Lower the Minimum Wage," *Wall Street Journal*, Oct. 9, 1976 (editorial), p. 18.

9. As reported in "A Carter Victory," *Wall Street Journal*, Nov. 3, 1977 (editorial), p. 20.

10. Paul A. Samuelson, *Economics: An Introductory Analysis*, 8th ed. (New York: McGraw-Hill, 1970), p. 372.

11. Finis Welch, "The Rising Impact of Minimum Wages," *Regulation* (Nov.–Dec. 1978), pp. 33–34.

12. J. R. Kearl, Clayne L. Pope, Gordon C. Whiting, and Larry T. Wimmer, "What Economists Think: A Confusion of Economists," *American Economic Review* (May 1979), pp. 28–37.

13. "Sense and Nonsense," *Wall Street Journal*, Aug. 15, 1977 (editorial), p. 12.

14. "Paying Fairer Dues in the South," *New York Times*, Aug. 20, 1977 (editorial), p. 20.

15. See letters to the editor by Rudy Oswald from the AFL-CIO and Clarence Mitchell from the Coalition for a Fair Minimum Wage under "No Job Loss in Raising the Minimum Wage," *New York Times*, Aug. 29, 1977, p. 26.

16. Ibid.

17. "Job Opportunities—for Children," *New York Times*, July 22, 1982 (editorial), p. 22.

18. Declaring this editorial to be "pop sociology," a letter writer responded that the country already had subminimum wages for many workers, called "interns" in congressional offices who work for far less than the minimum wage in order to gain relevant work experience. He proposed that the Reagan administration rename its proposal, "interns for business and get on with it" (Morton Lurie, "Subminimum Wage Is an Intern Program," *New York Times*, March 31, 1985 [letter to the editor], Sect. 4, p. 22).

19. See "A Garment Rule That Doesn't Fit," *New York Times*, May 23, 1981 (editorial), sect. I, p. 22; "A Stitch in Time," *New York Times*, Oct. 17, 1981, sect. I, p. 22; "Get Serious about Work at Home," *New York Times*, Nov. 14, 1984 (editorial), p. A34.

20. Sar A. Levitan and Isaac Shapiro, "The Minimum Wage: A Sinking Floor," *New York Times*, Jan. 16, 1986 (column), p. A23. However, the authors never pointed out that if that were true and if their proposed 30 percent increase in the minimum wage were passed, teenage employment would fall by 3 percent.

21. "Look: Liberalism!" *New York Times*, Feb. 15, 1987 (editorial), sect. IV, p. 20.

22. U.S. Senate, 100th Cong., 1st sess., *Minimum Wage Restoration Act of 1987* (March 25, 1987), p. 2.

23. "54 Economists Back Rise in Minimum Wage," *New York Times*, Feb. 24, 1988 (news article), sect. I, p. 24.

24. John Raisian and George J. Stigler, "Minimum Wage: A Perverse Policy," *New York Times*, Apr. 12, 1988 (column), sect. I, p. 35.

25. Kosters, "Minimum Wages: A Deeper Look at the '50s and '60," *Wall Street Journal*, 1989, p. 30. See also Kosters, *Jobs and the Minimum Wage: The Effect of Changes in the Level and Pattern of Coverage* (Washington, DC: American Enterprise Institute, 1989).

26. Arthur S. Flemming, "Raising Minimum Wage Increases Employment," *New York Times*, Mar. 4, 1988 (letter to the editor), p. 26.

27. Edward M. Kennedy, "Statement of Edward M. Kennedy upon Introduction of the Minimum Wage Restoration Act of 1987," U.S. Senate Office press release (March 25, 1987), p. 1.

28. "The Minimum Wage: A Better Way," *New York Times*, Sept. 21, 1988 (editorial), sect. I, p. 22. See also "Better Than $3.35, $4.25 or Even $5.05," *New York Times*, July 11, 1988 (editorial), sect. I, p. 16; "The Minimum Wage: A Detraction," *New York Times*, Mar. 22, 1989 (editorial), sect. I, p. 26; and "A Veto That Can Help the Poor," *New York Times*, June 15, 1989 (editorial), sect. I, p. 30.

29. "D.C.'s Maximum Minimum Wage," *Washington Post*, Oct. 11, 1991 (editorial), p. A26; "D.C.'s Killer Minimum Wage Law," *Washington Post*, Nov. 26, 1991 (editorial), p. A20; and "Minimum Wage Vs. Maximum Jobs," *Washington Post*, Dec. 5, 1991 (editorial), p. A22.

30. "The Inhuman Minimum," *Wall Street Journal*, Mar. 16, 1989 (editorial), p. A16.

31. "Minimum Wage, Maximum Hypocrisy," *Wall Street Journal*, Mar. 20, 1990 (editorial), p. A14.

32. Alan Reynolds, "Cruel Cost of the 1991 Minimum Wage," *Wall Street Journal*, July 7, 1992 (column), p. A12.

33. Lawrence Katz and Alan Krueger found in a study of fast-food restaurants in Texas that the 1990 and 1991 minimum-wage increases may have actually increased employment (Katz and Krueger, "The Effects of the Minimum Wage on the Fast-Food Industry," *Industrial and Labor Relations Review*, Oct. 1992, pp. 6–21). Their best explanation for their surprising findings is that the industry under study was monopsonistic. In another cross-sectional study of the effects of the federal minimum wage on teenage employment across states, economist David Card found that the 1990 increase in the minimum had no detectable employment effect ("Using Regional Variation in Wages to Measure the Effects of the Federal Minimum Wage," *Industrial and Labor Relations Review*, Oct. 1992, pp. 22–27). However, when the effects of minimum-wage increases are considered, David Neuman and William Wascher found a negative effect of the minimum wage on teenage employment similar in size to those found in much earlier studies ("Employment Effects of Minimum and Subminimum Wages: Panel Data on State Minimum Wage Laws," *Industrial and Labor Relations Review*, Oct. 1992, pp. 55–81). Janet Currie and Bruce Fallick in a panel study (using the National Lon-

gitudinal Survey of Youth) found that workers covered by the 1979 and 1980 minimum-wage increases were 3 to 4 percent less likely to be employed the following year. They also report finding no evidence that the minimum-wage increases affected the wages of workers who remained employed a year later ("A Note on the New Minimum Wage Research," [Los Angeles: Economics Department, University of California, Los Angeles, working paper, Mar. 1993]).

34. Steven Greenhouse, "Clinton Delays Push to Increase Minimum Wage," *New York Times*, June 6, 1993 (news article), p. A1.

35. Jerry Gray, "Trenton G.O.P. Accepts Minimum-Wage Phase-In," *New York Times*, Mar. 24, 1992 (news article), p. B5.

36. "Don't Sacrifice the Needy Workers," *New York Times*, June 7, 1993 (editorial), p. A14.

CHAPTER 6

Reflections on the Editorial Shifts

Charting the editorial position of one of the country's leading newspapers is a useful and interesting historical exercise. A review of the *Times* editorial position on the minimum wage helps document the major economic and ethical arguments that have guided the public policy debate on this topic during its stormy political history. Such an editorial review may also help explain why the nominal minimum and coverage have continued to rise over time and why the real minimum rose through 1968 and has fallen (irregularly) since. Coverage appears to have been extended for humanitarian and economic reasons. Extended coverage would, as the editors noted, moderate labor market discrimination caused by the minimum and would impair the "unfair" competition of uncovered workers; it would also enhance the competitive position of workers earning more than the minimum and of firms—especially northern firms—that must pay more than the minimum.

From a reading of the minimum-wage history, as reported in news accounts and editorials of the *Times*, it appears that increases were, at times, moderated or postponed in what amounted to political deals to extend coverage. At the same time, extended coverage increased the unemployment impact of any given rise in the minimum, a point that, as noted, Marvin Kosters has stressed.[1] Decreases in the real minimum after 1968 also appear to have been a part of political trades for extended coverage. The proponents of the minimum-wage increase appear to have been seeking some "acceptable" level of job losses created by combined adjustments in the real minimum and its coverage.[2]

The reasons for changes in the editorial position of a major newspaper are not always apparent, especially when the editors do not even acknowledge that their paper's position has changed, as the *Times* editors did not. Answers to exactly why the editors switched stances thus must be somewhat speculative. One obvious explanation may involve changes in key members of the newspaper's editorial board. I have noted that changes in key leadership positions did occur the year before the *Times* switched its position in 1977. (Changes in editorial writers could not be determined.)

However, while never unimportant in explaining editorial positions of a newspaper, personnel changes may be less a real cause and merely a more apparent explanation of any switch in editorial position. Major editorial positions at the *New York Times,* as at most of the country's other major papers, are determined by a committee. In such an environment, one or several changes in the editorial board's composition may or may not have been the crucial reason for change, because changes in personalities do not necessarily involve changes in the ideology or analytical skills of the editorial writers. A central task of the editorial committee must be to provide, as far as practical, some consistency in editorial position; editorial boards are not completely free to reverse adopted positions simply because particular personalities have departed or joined the board. In 1977, the switch to opposition was the product of some evolutionary movement within the *Times* related to its position on the minimum; actually, the switch followed on the heels of efforts by the editors to temper the impact of the minimum wage by promoting increases to "sensible" levels and by implementation of a subminimum. Only those employed at the *Times* during that period could offer somewhat accurate insights into the impact of personnel changes.[3]

From the vantage point of this editorial review, it appears that the changes in the *Times* editorial positions on the minimum wage may not have resulted so much from changes in the ideological leanings of the editorial board as they did to consequences of very realistic assessments of the "preponderance of the evidence," or the lack thereof, on the employment effects of the minimum wage. The first switch from staunch opposition to virtually complete support that occurred in 1950 was guided, so it appears, by a lack of evidence on job losses. In the late 1940s, the editors must have felt that by continuing to harp on the potential job losses from minimum-wage increases, they had been crying "wolf" for a decade or more. There was simply not much credible evidence around to support continued opposition. Employment in most industrial categories was rising during the war and postwar years faster than most economists and policymakers had believed could happen, given the required massive shift from the production of military hardware to consumer and investment goods in the postwar years. Indeed, many expected a recession.

Furthermore, in the late 1940s the science of econometrics was still in its infancy, and the few economists who had the requisite statistical skills did not yet have access to the computer power necessary to yield useful statistical conclusions. Such investigations might have helped to disentangle the actual effects of minimum-wage increases from the myriad other forces that were expanding or contracting job opportunities in the 1940s. The most influential study on the effects of the minimum from the 1950s was one done by the Labor Department (released after the *Times* had shifted its support), and it showed little or no effect. This is probably because the study was undertaken for an increase that was effective in the midst of an expansion (the unemployment rate fell from 5.5 percent in 1950 to 2.2 percent in 1952) and possibly because the study was done at the behest of Eisenhower's labor department secretary, who was committed to raising the minimum and extending its coverage.

In addition, in the late 1940s, the minimum wage applied mainly to industries whose lowest wages were typically already above the legal minimum (e.g., to manufacturing and interstate transportation) and to only a minor portion of all of the country's low-wage workers.[4] Such facts imply that the minimum-wage increases in 1939, 1945, and 1950 may have affected the employment of too few workers to be detected—even if there had not been the widely unexpected postwar boom.

Over the next two decades, however, evidence on the adverse effects of the minimum wage mounted. Casual observation of the growing gap between the unemployment rates of black and white male teenagers plotted in Figure 4.1 and the close (almost cozy) relationship between the real minimum and the relative teenage unemployment rate plotted in Figure 5.1 must have, from time to time, caught the attention of the *Times* editors. By the late 1960s, the cost of computing power had fallen dramatically, making it more widely available and facilitating the increased use of econometrics to analyze labor market issues, including the minimum wage. By the mid-1970s, economists had substantiated impressions drawn from the data shown in Figures 4.1 and 5.1 and had effectively undercut practically every *economic* (as distinguished from *political*) argument that the *New York Times* and other national newspapers could use to promote further increases. By the time the editors had switched back to opposition in early 1977, the minimum had been shown to be anti-South, antiteenagers, antiblack, antielderly, and antiwoman.[5]

Such findings must have caused the *Times* editorial board consternation, since in the 1960s the *Times* had been a media leader in the national political campaign to expand civil rights for blacks and women. By the late 1970s, some scholarly works and professional discussions were under way that showed that low-wage workers who retained their jobs in the face of a minimum-wage increase might suffer a net welfare loss because the mandated increase in their money wage might be offset by employers cutting on-the-job training and fringe benefits.[6] This argument was never mentioned, however, in *Times* editorials.

The widespread findings of job losses due to minimum-wage increases that were reported in the 1970s may have been the product of more diligent efforts by economic researchers who had more sophisticated statistical techniques at their disposal. However, the growing evidence on job losses may also have been more easily picked up in econometric studies because, since the 1950s, the coverage of the minimum wage had been greatly extended, and any given increase in the minimum could affect more people. The number of job losses may have simply grown to the point that they could no longer be readily dismissed. The "high-tech" econometric research, however, probably had much less impact on the *Times* minimum-wage position than did two other types of "low-tech" descriptive data: (1) the obvious and dramatic divergence in the unemployment rates of black and white male teenagers, and (2) the simple, widely reported observation that 40 percent of teenage minimum-wage workers "live with families whose incomes exceed $15,000 per year" (or 11 percent above the median-family income in 1977), along with the finding that "five out of six jobs paying the minimum wage are not held by poor people at all, but by teenage children of middle-income families or by second earners in families with few children" (more recent calculations of economists at the Urban Institute) (Sept. 21, 1988). The several changes in key personnel may have given the *Times* editorial board a convenient excuse to "go with the flow" of the mounting adverse employment evidence.

Still, the voting public and their political leaders did not appear, as yet, to agree fully with the assessments of minimum-wage evidence by most economists and the *Times* editors. In November 1989, the 1990 and 1991 increases in the minimum were approved by overwhelming majorities by both houses of Congress and signed into law by President Bush, who, it might be mentioned in passing, liked to advertise his conservatism and his allegiance to reliance on markets. Most of the measure's supporters in Congress appear to have agreed that the increases would cause job losses, especially among teenagers and minorities. I have noted that President Carter's secretary of labor admitted, in 1976, that the then proposed increases would destroy jobs. In fact, proponents have continued to willingly acknowledge the potential for job losses. In 1986, two ardent minimum-wage supporters—Sar Levitan and Isaac Shapiro—sought a minimum of $4.33 an hour "because that is a level where *only a few jobs are lost* but where income and work incentives are substantial."[7] Furthermore, by 1989, it appeared that the real minimum had sunk so low that it affected very few workers, making an increase politically acceptable. In sharp contrast to calculations seven years earlier,[8] researchers figured in 1989 that a 10 percent increase in the minimum might reduce teenage employment by 0.6 percent (meaning that the proposed 27 percent increase in the minimum wage by 1991 would reduce teenage employment "by fewer than 100,000").[9]

Thus, in 1989, the minimum-wage debate had become a throwback to the "efficiency versus equity" debate that has long haunted public policy controversies. The *Times* editors sided explicitly with the prevailing opinion in the economics profession. However, unlike the *Times* and the vast majority of economists, members of Congress appear to have passed additional minimum-wage increases because they saw the expected "modest" increases in unemployment as a necessary social, political, and economic cost of accomplishing with one bill a triple-edged political goal that had always accompanied the minimum wage debate: (1) improving the living standards for close to 4 million workers—regardless of their families' incomes; (2) impairing the competitiveness of low-wage workers and the firms that would otherwise continue to employ people at "substandard" or "exploitive" wage rates; and (3) reducing the need for government welfare expenditures.

In general, the *New York Times* association with the minimum wage has had a turbulent but honorable history. From all appearances, the paper's stances have been guided more by a search for the expected and observed employment effects and better policy alternatives than by unthinking or rigid ideology. Its editorials on the first minimum-wage bill could not have been more sophisticated (or attuned to the prevailing economic theories of the day). The editors' willingness to cite computed "elasticity coefficients" in 1938 is an obvious testimonial to the level of sophistication their initial editorials reached (a level that, it might be noted, has not been equaled since). The editors lapsed into blatant demagoguery, without references to logic or facts, during a relatively short period in the late 1960s and the very early 1970s. But they reversed their position on the minimum, for the most part, when the available evidence (in the late 1940s, the evidence was, indeed, scarce) would no longer support their old stance.

The one consistent thread that runs through all *Times* editorials has been a concern for the truly needy. In calling for the elimination of the minimum wage in 1987, the *Times* editors never challenged the social objectives of the advocates of the minimum, just the consequences of the methods proposed in the name of the poor.

Notes

1. See Kosters, "Minimum Wages: A Deeper Look at the '50s and '60," *Wall Street Journal,* Oct. 19, 1987 (column), p. 30; and Marvin Kosters, *Jobs and the Minimum Wage: The Effect of Changes in the Level and Pattern of Coverage,* (Washington, DC: American Enterprise Institute, 1989).
2. This is a preliminary conclusion that the author draws from empirical work currently under way with William Chapel on the political and economic determinants of the real minimum wage (University of Mississippi, Department of Economics and Finance).
3. Several requests were made concerning personnel changes at the *Times* since the late 1930s. No response was received.
4. See Kosters, *Jobs and the Minimum Wage,* pp. 8–29.
5. Again, for a review of much of the literature developed in the 1960s and 1970s, see Charles Brown, Curtis Gilroy, and Andrew Cohen, "The Effect of the Minimum Wage on Employment and Unemployment," *Journal of Economic Literature,* (June 1982), pp. 487–528. In particular, see Marvin Kosters and Finis Welch, "The Effects of the Minimum Wage by Race, Sex, and Age," *Racial Discrimination in Economic Life,* edited by Anthony Pascal (Lexington, MA: Heath, 1972) pp. 103–108.
6. This unconventional view of the minimum wage is presented in greater detail in Chapter 9. See also Walter J. Wessels, *Minimum Wages, Fringe Benefits, and Working Conditions* (Washington, DC: American Enterprise Institute, 1981).
7. Sar A. Levitan and Isaac Shapiro, "The Minimum Wage: A Sinking Floor," *New York Times,* Jan. 16, 1986 (column), p. 19 (emphasis added).
8. See Brown, Gilroy, and Cohen, "The Effect of the Minimum Wage on Employment and Unemployment."
9. From the work of Alison Wellington at the University of Michigan, as reported in Peter Passell, "Economic Scene: Minimum Wage: A Reality Test," *New York Times,* Mar. 15, 1989 (news report), sect. IV, p. 2.

PART II

THE ECONOMICS OF
THE MINIMUM WAGE

CHAPTER 7

The Conventional Economic View of Minimum-Wage Laws

Economists traditionally have argued that minimum-wage increases reduce employment in competitive markets, thereby increasing the welfare of those low-skilled workers who remain employed but decreasing the welfare of others who lose their jobs (who may remain unemployed or accept less gainful employment in areas of the economy where minimum-wage regulations are not applied). Also, economists point out that the minimum wage can increase the crime rate. How is it that economists reach such conclusions?

The Market Consequences of Minimum Wages

Consider Figure 7.1, which depicts a downward-sloping demand curve for low-skilled labor and an upward-sloping supply curve of low-skilled labor. The downward-sloping demand curve implies that employers will hire more workers (everything else constant) at a lower wage than a higher one, and they will respond to the wage rate for several reasons. First, profit-maximizing employers will tend to expand production until the marginal contribution of additional workers begins to diminish, which implies that within the relevant range of production, additional workers will be worth (in terms of the market value of the product they can produce) progressively less as more are hired. Second, lower wages can inspire a substitution of low-skilled workers for other resources used in production, such as higher-skilled workers and expensive equipment. Third, lower wages imply lower costs and prices for the product produced, which can inspire more sales and lead, in turn, to a greater need for workers to satisfy the additional quantity demanded.

The upward-sloping curve that represents the supply of labor implies that the wage must be raised to attract additional workers. The main

FIGURE 7.1 Equilibrium in the labor market

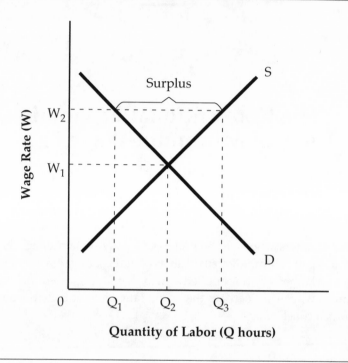

reason given for the slope of the curve is that the value of the economic opportunities different workers have at their disposal vary across workers. Some workers have high-valued opportunities, while the opportunities available for others may have little or no value. Any given wage will attract those workers into the market whose alternative opportunities generally are lower than that wage rate. The wage offered in low-skilled (or any other) labor market must be progressively raised to offset the progressively higher-valued opportunities the additional workers must forgo.

If the market is competitive and free of government intervention, the wage rate will settle, as shown in Figure 7.1, at the intersection of the supply and demand curves, or at W_1. (A wage above W_1 would indicate that more workers are seeking jobs than there are jobs available and that competitive pressure would push the wage down. A wage below W_1 would imply that more workers are demanded than there are those willing to work at the going wage and that there is upward competitive pressure on the wage.) Suppose, however, that politicians consider that market wage, W_1, too low to provide a decent living and pass a law requiring employers to pay no less than W_2. The law reduces employment, because employers will not be able to afford, given worker productivity and reduced sales, to employ as many people, and the quantity of labor demanded will fall from Q_2 to Q_1.

As the argument is normally developed by economists, those who manage to keep their jobs at the minimum wage will be better off (their take-home pay will increase from W_1 to W_2). Others, however, will no longer have jobs and will either become permanently unemployed or settle for work in different, lower paying, or less desirable labor markets. If the minimum wage displaces them from their preferred employment, their full wage rate—that is, their money wage plus the nonmonetary benefits of their jobs—will have been reduced. For those who become permanently unemployed, their money wage will drop from a level that minimum-wage supporters judged to be unacceptable to zero.

To make matters worse, when a minimum wage is introduced, more workers are willing to work (see Figure 7.1). Workers with jobs paying W_1, and who have fewer opportunities at W_2, must now compete with an influx of other workers.

Certainly there are some theoretical objections to the model just presented, and these will be discussed in Chapter 8. Almost all of the empirical studies done over the past three decades, however, support the gloomy predictions of the model (which is the position adopted by the editors of the *New York Times*).[1] In 1969, two scholars concluded:

> The impression created in most government studies that federal minimum wage policy has produced no adverse effects is erroneous. . . . Minimum wage rates produce gains for some groups of workers at the expense of those that are the least favored in terms of marketable skills or location.[2]

Other researchers observed that minimum-wage laws have tended to destabilize employment among workers covered by such laws, particularly nonwhites and young people.[3] When the demand for goods and services falls, employers cannot lower prices to boost sales because their wages cannot drop below the minimum. Instead, the employers are forced to adjust to changing market conditions by reducing employment.

A 1977 study corroborates these findings. Minimum-wage legislation was found to hurt teenagers—especially those who were nonwhite males. Specifically, with the boost in the minimum from $1.25 in 1966 to $1.60 in 1972, employment among teenagers fell by 3.8 percent.[4]

Economists probably have understated the adverse consequences of the minimum wage for the targeted groups of workers by making the common presumption that low-skilled workers who retain their jobs are "better off." However, as argued in Chapter 9, employers may respond to a higher minimum by reducing fringe benefits (to the extent that they exist) and by increasing the work demands on covered workers. Economists also commonly presume that the workers who have the jobs after the minimum wage is imposed, Q_1, represent a subgroup of the workers who had the jobs, Q_2, when the wage was determined strictly by the forces of supply and demand, but this is unlikely since the minimum wage will attract additional workers, $Q_3 - Q_2$, into the market. Some, perhaps most, of these additional workers will be more productive than those who were in the market when the wage was W_1, as evidenced by the fact that they have been positioned farther up the supply curve and have had higher-valued opportunities elsewhere. In short, many, if not all, of the workers who have jobs at W_1 can be expected either to withdraw from the market or to be supplanted by new arrivals who have been induced to enter the market by the higher wage.

Social and Nonmonetary Effects of Minimum Wage Laws

Economists maintain that minimum-wage laws also have several social effects that often are overlooked. By increasing unemployment, minimum-wage laws increase the number of people receiving public assistance and unemployment compensation. (Proponents of the minimum wage argue the opposite, i.e., that the minimum reduces the need for welfare by raising the income of low-skilled workers above the poverty level.) The laws may also account for increases in some criminal activity, since the unemployed who lack opportunities in the legitimate labor market may see crime as an alternative to employment (indeed, crime is a form of employment). The larger labor pool that develops when a minimum wage increases competition for jobs is likely to harbor potential for increased discrimination on the basis of sex, race, or religion.

The Political Support for Minimum Wage Laws

Why do minimum-wage laws attract so much political support? Part of the reason may be that the general public is largely unaware of their negative effects. Many forces operate on the labor market, making it almost impossible for the average person to single out the effects of one law. Few give enough thought to the idea of a minimum wage adversely affecting employment opportunities. Those on whom the burden of these laws falls hardest—that is, young, relatively unproductive workers, many of whom cannot vote—are least likely to understand the negative effects. The people who retain their jobs at the higher wage are visible members of the work force; those who lose their jobs are often far less visible, concentrated in urban ghettos.

Another reason minimum-wage laws attract political support is that they benefit those who retain their jobs and receive higher paychecks. Many college students favor the minimum wage, perhaps because they expect and are expected to be more productive than less educated members of their generation. They therefore may regard it as less likely that they will lose their jobs as a result of the legislation; also, they may find the low-skilled jobs more attractive once the minimum wage is in force. Labor unions also have an incentive to support minimum-wage laws; unions are in a better bargaining position when the government raises wages in nonunion sectors of the economy. Under such circumstances, union wage demands are not as likely to prompt employers to move into nonunionized sectors of the economy. In fact, as was argued by the *Times* editors in 1937 when the federal minimum wage was originally proposed, the first minimum wage would retard the exodus of firms and jobs to the nonunionized South from the unionized North. The introduction of the minimum wage reduced the net benefit of moving south, slowing the exodus.

Notes

1. For a review of the economic literature on the minimum wage through the early 1980s, see Charles Brown, Curtis Gilroy, and Andrew Cohen, "The Effect of the Minimum Wage on Employment and Unemployment," *Journal of Economic Literature* (June 1982), pp. 487–528.
2. John M. Peterson and Charles T. Stewart, *Employment Effects of Minimum Wage Rates* (Washington, DC: American Enterprise Institute for Public Policy Research, 1969), pp. 151–155.
3. Marvin Kosters and Finis Welch, "The Effects of Minimum Wages on the Distribution of Changes in Aggregate Employment," *American Economic Review 62* (June 1972), pp. 323–331.
4. James F. Ragan, "Minimum Wages and the Youth Labor Market," *Review of Economics and Statistics 59* (May 1977), pp. 129–136.

CHAPTER 8

The Monopsonistic Employer and the Minimum Wage

Probably the most theoretically sound and, thus, very persistent argument in favor of the minimum wage is provided by the fact that labor markets are never as competitive as economists assume when they develop a case against the minimum (see Chapter 7). Indeed, proponents maintain that many employers are in markets where they have significant *monopsony* power, meaning they individually are capable of affecting the going wage rate in their markets by their decisions on how many workers to hire. As the late economist George Stigler argued (and as mentioned earlier), it can be expected that some monopsonistic employers will (up to some limit) actually increase their employment in the face of an increase in the minimum wage.

Market Power and the Minimum Wage

Power is never complete or absolute. It is always circumscribed by limitations of knowledge and the forces of law, custom, and the market. Within limits, employers can hire, fire, and decide what products to produce and what type of labor to employ. Laws restrict the conditions of employment (working hours, working environment) they may offer. Competition imposes additional constraints. In a highly competitive labor market, an employer who offers very low wages will be outbid by others vying for the same workers. Competition for labor pushes wages up to a certain level (W_1 in Figure 7.1), forcing some employers to withdraw from the market but permitting others to hire at the going wage rate.[1]

For the individual employer, then, the freedom of the competitive market is highly constrained. However, for those lucky employers who enjoy the power of a monopsony, the market constraints are not so

81

binding. The term *monopsony* is used most frequently to indicate the sole or dominant employer of labor in a given market. (Monopsony should not be confused with monopoly, the single *seller* of a good or service.) A good example of a monopsony would be a large coal mining company in a small town with no other industry. A firm that is not a sole employer but that dominates the market for a certain type of labor is said to have monopsony power, which is the ability of a producer to alter the price of a resource (in this case, labor) by changing the quantity employed. By reducing competition for workers' services, monopsony power allows employers to suppress the wage rate below competitive levels. Why is this so?

The Cost of Labor

As in the previous analysis, let us assume that the downward-sloping demand curve D in Figure 8.1 shows the market demand for workers and that the upward-sloping supply curve S shows the number of workers willing to work at various wage rates. If all firms act independently—that is, if they compete with one another—the market wage rate will settle at W_2, and the number of workers hired will be Q_2. At lower wage rates, such as W_1, shortages will develop. As indicated by the market demand curve, employers will be willing to pay more than W_1. If a shortage exists, the market wage will be bid up to W_2.

An increase in the wage rate will encourage more workers to seek jobs. The competitive bidding, however, imposes costs on employers. The firm that offers a wage higher than W_1 forces every other firm to offer a comparable wage to retain its current employees. If a firm wants to acquire additional workers, it must offer an even higher wage. As they bid the wage up, firms impose reciprocal costs on one another, as at an auction.

Because any increase in the wage paid to one worker must be extended to all, the total cost to all employers of hiring even one worker at a higher rate can be substantial. If the wage rises from W_1 to W_2, as shown in Figure 8.1, the total wage bill for the first Q_1 workers rises by the wage increase ($W_2 - W_1$) times Q_1 workers. Table 8.1 shows how the effect of a wage increase is multiplied when it must be extended to other workers. The first two columns reflect the assumption that more workers will accept jobs as the wage rate rises. If only one worker is demanded, he or she can be hired for $20,000. The firm's total wage bill will also be $20,000 (column 3). If two workers are demanded and the second worker will not work for less than $22,000, the salary of the first worker must be

FIGURE 8.1 The competitive labor market

Quantity of Workers (Q)

raised to $22,000. That brings the cost of the second worker to $24,000 (column 4): $22,000 for his or her services plus the $2,000 raise that must be given to the first worker.

The cost of additional workers can be similarly derived. When the sixth worker is added, he or she must be offered $30,000, and the five previously hired workers must each be given a $2,000 raise. The cost of adding this new worker, called the marginal cost of labor, has risen to $40,000. Note that the gap between the marginal cost of labor and the going wage rate expands as the number of workers hired increases. When two workers are hired, the gap is $2,000 ($24,000 – $22,000). When six are employed, it is $10,000 ($40,000 – $30,000).

Figure 8.2, based on columns 1 and 4 of Table 8.1, provides a graphic representation of the marginal cost of labor. The marginal cost curve lies above the supply curve, because the actual costs of hiring a new worker (beyond the first worker) are greater than that worker's salary.

FIGURE 8.2 The marginal cost of labor

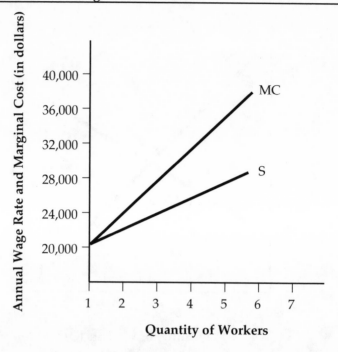

TABLE 8.1 The marginal cost of labor

Number of Workers Willing to Work (1)	Annual Wage of Each Worker (2)	Total Wage Bill (1) x (2) (3)	Marginal Cost of Additional Worker [Change in (3)] (4)
1	$20,000	$20,000	$20,000
2	22,000	44,000	24,000
3	24,000	72,000	28,000
4	26,000	104,000	32,000
5	28,000	140,000	36,000
6	30,000	180,000	40,000

FIGURE 8.3 The monopsonist's wage rate and the minimum wage

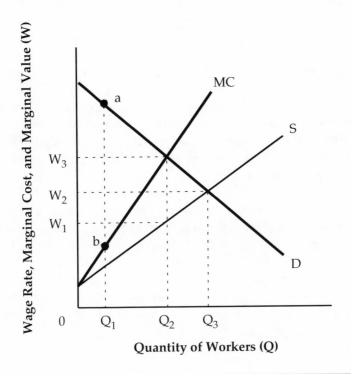

The Monopsonistic Hiring Decision

The monopsonistic employer does not get caught in the competitive bind, by definition being the only or dominant employer. The monopsonist can search through the various wage–quantity combinations on the labor supply curve for the one that maximizes profits. The monopsonist will keep hiring more workers as long as their contribution to revenues is greater than their additional costs, as shown by the marginal cost of labor curve *MC* in Figure 8.3. To maximize profits, in other words, the monopsonist will hire until the marginal cost of the last worker hired equals his or her marginal value, as shown by the market demand curve for labor. Given the demand for labor *D*, the monopsonist's optimal employment level will be Q_2, where the marginal cost and demand for labor curves intersect. Note that that employment level is lower than the competitive employment level, Q_3.

Why hire where marginal cost equals marginal value? Suppose the monopsonist employed fewer workers—say Q_1. The marginal value of worker Q_1 would be quite high (point *a*), while his or her marginal cost would be low (point *b*). The monopsonist would be forgoing profits by hiring only Q_1 workers. Beyond Q_2 workers, the reverse would be true. The marginal cost of each new worker would be greater than his or her marginal value. Hiring more than Q_2 workers would reduce profits.

Once a monopsonist has chosen the employment level Q_2, it will pay workers no more than is required by the labor supply curve S. In Figure 8.3, the monopsonist must pay only W_1—much less than the wage that would be paid in a competitive labor market, W_2. In other words, the monopsonist hires fewer workers and pays them less than an employer in a competitive labor market.

It is the monopsonistic firm's power to reduce the number of workers it hires that enables it to hold wages below the competitive level. In a competitive labor market, if one firm attempts to cut employment and reduce wages, it will not be able to keep its business going, for workers will depart to other employers willing to pay the going market wage. The individual firm in a competitive market is not large enough in relation to the entire labor market to exercise monopsony power. It therefore must reluctantly accept the market wage W_2 as a given.

The Employment Consequences
of the Minimum Wage

Now, suppose a minimum wage is imposed on the monopsony employer at W_2 (the competitive wage level), thus raising the workers' wage rate from W_1. Instead of the employment level going down, it will go up. Given the minimum-wage rate, the marginal cost of labor curve is no longer relevant (because employers can no longer choose to lower the wage below the minimum of W_2). The marginal cost of each unit of labor is now the minimum wage W_2, which means that the employer will extend employment from Q_2 to Q_3. The marginal cost of each additional worker up to Q_3 is then lower than the value of each additional worker (as indicated by the demand curve). The minimum wage does not change the fundamental profit-maximizing drive of monopsonistic employers, though it does change the way they look at the cost of each worker—the net effect of which is that more workers are hired.

A Word of Caution

Few economists dispute the validity of the foregoing argument. They simply note that there are limits above which the minimum wage cannot be increased without giving rise to a reduction in employment within monopsony markets. If the minimum wage is pushed above W_3 in Figure 8.3, notice that employment will fall below the monopsony level Q_2. (For example, if the wage is raised to point a, then employment will fall to Q_1.)

Economists also question whether monopsonies are sufficiently pervasive in low-skilled markets to nullify the essential conclusions drawn from a model of competitive labor markets. As noted earlier, the empirical work strongly indicates that any increase in employment by monopsonies (if they exist with any significant market power) is more than offset by a reduction in employment within the competitive markets. In essence, this is the general position adopted by the *Times* editors in the late 1970s; they deduced that, in the case of the minimum wage, as in most matters of public policies, there are pluses and minuses, but the minuses tend to outweigh the pluses (or the job losses in competitive labor markets outweigh the job gains in monopsony markets).

Note

1. Competitors who do not hire influence the wage rate just as much as those who do; their presence on the sidelines keep prices from falling. If a firm lowers its wages, other employers may move into the market and hire away part of the work force.

CHAPTER 9

Nonconventional Consequences of the Minimum Wage

The conventional line of analysis and policy proposals relating to the market consequences of the minimum wage (developed in Chapter 7) misses several important but relatively simple points, the most important of which is that the minimum wage does not necessarily make a significant share of the targeted workers better off. Moreover, the analysis leads to the conclusion that minimum-wage increases should not be expected to have substantial adverse employment effects in most low-skill labor markets, primarily because employers can be expected to adjust to the added labor costs of the minimum wage by lowering the nonwage benefits of employment or increasing the work demands imposed on covered workers. The analysis that follows helps explain why studies have generally found that a 10 percent increase in the minimum wage can be expected to reduce employment by as little as 1 to 3 percent.[1] As noted earlier, this is a line of argument that the *Times* editors have chosen not to use. However, this new line of analysis fortifies the case against the minimum wage. It suggests that if the editors got their way and the minimum wage were reduced to zero, targeted workers would, indeed, be made better off.

The Complexity of Employment Contracts

By its very nature, employment in any labor market is a complex phenomenon. Employment is based on a great variety of potential contract terms and a tremendous assortment of environmental conditions. The money-wage rate paid workers is only one of many, many dimensions of work. To develop the analysis in its starkest terms, consider employers who are interested in draining as much profit as possible from their workers and who, therefore, pay as little as possible.

Such profit-maximizing employers will, before settling on wage offers to workers, consider the entire work situation with the objective of minimizing costs and maximizing output. As is fully recognized in much highly sophisticated labor market theory, employers can be expected to seek a combination of capital (plant and machinery) and labor that results in the most profits. In addition, they will seek to adjust all the implicit and explicit terms of the labor contract and the environmental conditions of the workplace to maximize the efficiency of labor, given the capital that is employed, and to minimize the *effective* total wage, including the money wage that may be paid on an hourly basis and the nonmonetary benefits of the workplace environment.[2]

In less technical terms, employers can effectively pay workers with dollars, with normal fringe benefits such as prepaid medical care, and with pleasant working conditions that may arise from the installation of air conditioning, noise abatement systems, or those informal musical programs broadcast throughout the workplace. Workers can also be effectively paid with a convenient workplace location, chances for on-the-job training, and fair production demands of supervisors.

To achieve maximum efficiency and profits from a given expenditure level, the last dollar of cost incurred on, say, air conditioning (or any other fringe benefit or condition of work) must reduce the money-wage bill or raise company revenues by one dollar. If this marginal condition does not prevail, then employers can either cut their expenditures on air conditioning and reduce labor cost or they can increase output with the same labor cost. Employers should, on the margin, be indifferent to spending an additional dollar on wages, on air conditioning, or on some other condition of work.

Employers' expenditures on different working conditions or fringe benefits will have different effects on supply of, and demand for, labor. Expenditures on, for example, company picnics may not affect worker productivity. However, since picnics can increase the supply of workers, such expenditures can be offset by a reduction in the money-wage bill. Profit-maximizing employers will extend the expenditures on picnics up to the point that the last dollar of cost incurred will be just offset by a dollar reduction in the total wage bill that is due to an increase in the supply of labor.

Worker productivity can be increased by changes in working conditions or fringe benefits, for instance, by the introduction of air conditioning. A firm will increase its expenditures on air conditioning until the additional cost equals the additional revenue received by the improvement in productivity plus the reduction in the wage bill. Since each worker will be worth more in terms of output per worker-hour and receive less in money wages, the number of workers demanded should increase and the firm should be willing to hire more workers at any given wage rate.

When workers' productivity rises due to a change in the workplace or fringe benefits, the firm's supply of labor may increase or decrease, depending on how the change affects workers' job satisfaction. If the work experience is made more satisfying, more workers should be willing to work for any given wage, that is, labor supply should increase. For similar reasons, the supply of labor should contract with workplace changes that reduce workers' job-related satisfaction. The important points to remember are thus:

⊃ An increase in the labor supply can be expected to lead to a reduction in the wage rate paid.

⊃ A decrease in the labor supply can be expected to lead to an increase in the wage rate paid.

This means that when the supply of labor increases, the cost of the change in workplace conditions can be offset by an increase in the productivity of labor or by a reduction in the wage that the firm would otherwise have to pay. Alternatively, the supply of workers may be reduced by the workplace change initiated by the employer. However, the change will still be made as long as it adds more to revenue than it adds to cost.

It is also possible that the profit-maximizing employer could voluntarily (i.e., without any government encouragement or requirement) make changes in the workplace that reduce the productivity of labor but increase the supply of labor. As long as the reduction in the value of worker productivity lost is less than the reduction in the wage bill, the change is profitable for the firm. Reducing the production demands on employees might also reduce productivity and the market value of workers—hence, the supply of labor—and therefore reduce the firm's wage bill.

The central point of the foregoing discussion is that given all the possible changes that can be made, profit-maximizing employers will make those changes that enable them to minimize their labor costs and maximize profits. Indeed, firms in competitive markets will be forced to find a cost-minimizing combination of capital, labor, fringe benefits, and working conditions. If employers in a competitive labor market do not achieve the cost-minimizing combination, they will be underpriced and forced to contract their position or withdraw from the final product market.

The Impact of Minimum Wages

Minimum-wage laws establish a legal floor for *money wages*; however, they do not suppress competitive pressures. These restrictions only cap the pressures in one of the multitude of competitive outlets, namely, money wages. More to the point, they do not set a legal minimum for the *effective wage* (including the money and nonmoney benefits of employment) that is paid to workers.

The impact of mandating minimum wages depends on the ability of the employer to adjust the nonmoney conditions of work or fringe benefits in response to a required pay change. The conventional analysis of minimum-wage laws in economics textbooks implicitly assumes that money wages are the only form of labor compensation. Thus, when the money wage is set at a legal minimum, employment falls by some amount given by the demand for labor.

Consider the impact of wages in the standard supply and demand graph in Figure 9.1, which has the workers' wage rate on the vertical axis and the quantity of labor (or number of workers) on the horizontal axis. The demand for labor curve, labeled D_1, is downward sloping in accordance with reasoned argument (implicit in the foregoing discussion) that employers will hire more workers if the wage is reduced. A decrease in the wage rate from W_m to W_0 will lead to an increase in the number of workers hired from Q_1 to Q_2. In contrast, the supply of labor curve labeled S_1 is upward sloping in accordance with the argument that more workers will be willing to work at higher than at lower wages. Therefore, an increase in the wage rate from W_0 to W_m will lead to an increase in the number of workers willing to work from Q_1 to Q_2.

If an acceptable minimum wage is set at W_m in Figure 9.1, the quantity of labor demanded falls from Q_2 to Q_1 and the quantity of labor supplied expands from Q_2 to Q_3. According to the conventional view, a surplus of unemployed labor emerges in the market equal to $Q_3 - Q_1$. This is because there is no assumed way employers can react to that surplus of unemployed labor. From this line of analysis, the conclusion is that the effective wage for those who retain their jobs rises by the amount of the increase in their wage rate—the competitive market wage rate W_0 minus the minimum wage, W_m. The people who lose their jobs are pushed into lower-paying labor markets or onto the roles of the unemployed.

This line of analysis may still be fully applicable to those few labor markets in which money is the only form of compensation and in which employers can do little or nothing to change the skill and production demands imposed on workers. In such cases, minimum-wage laws may

FIGURE 9.1 The conventional view of minimum-wage laws

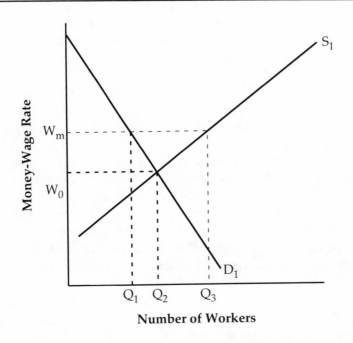

Number of Workers

still have the predicted effect: a labor market surplus of unemployed menial workers caused by an above-market level of compensation.

However, the previous analysis does not consider the possibility that profit-maximizing competitive employers will adjust to the labor market surplus created by the minimum-wage law. It seems highly reasonable that employers who are capable of paying wages that are "too low," because of, for example, antisocial attitudes or competitive pressures, are also quite capable of adjusting other conditions of work in response to the labor market surplus. Indeed, to remain cost-competitive, employers in competitive labor markets will have to adjust to the labor surplus by cutting labor costs in nonwage ways—for example, by eliminating workplace picnics, reducing fringe benefits, or increasing production demands.[3] Such employers can be expected to reduce their nonmoney labor costs until they are no longer confronted by a surplus—that is, until their labor markets clear once again.[4] That being said, the labor market effects of employers' nonmoney adjustments made in response to a wage minimum can be discussed briefly in terms of two general cases.

Case I: Changes in Fringe Benefits
that Do Not Affect Labor Productivity

Employers can be expected to respond to a minimum-wage law by cutting or eliminating those fringe benefits and conditions of work, like workplace parties, that increase the supply of labor but do not materially affect labor productivity. By reducing such nonmoney benefits of employment, the labor costs are reduced from what they would otherwise have been and nothing is lost in the way of reduced labor productivity.

Continuation of such nonmoney benefits as affect the supply is made uneconomical by the money-wage minimum; they no longer pay for themselves in terms of lower wage rates. Furthermore, employers in highly competitive final products markets must adjust such work conditions to remain competitive and survive. Otherwise, other firms will lower their labor costs (by contracting or by eliminating fringe benefits) and force the employers who retain their fringe benefits and continue to pay the higher minimum-wage rate out of their final product markets.

Because of the changes in the work conditions, the supply curve of labor (the position of which is partially determined by working conditions and fringe benefits) can be expected to shift upward. The effects of such a supply shift are shown in Figure 9.2, which incorporates the supply and demand curves of the preceding figure.

The vertical shift in the supply curve will be equal to labor's dollar evaluation, on the margin, of the adjustments made in employment conditions. The demand curve for labor will shift upward to the right, reflecting the reduced expenditure per unit of labor on fringe benefits.[5]

As before, fringe benefits are provided as long as their cost to the firm per unit of labor is less than the reduced wage rate—so long as labor's evaluation of the fringe benefits lost is greater than the firm's costs. Therefore, the vertical, upward shift in the supply curve will be greater than the vertical, upward shift in the demand curve. In Figure 9.2, the vertical shift in the supply curve is ac, and the vertical shift in the demand curve is less, ab.[6] It is important to note that the market clears at the minimum wage, however, because of secondary market adjustments in fringe benefits. But it is equally important to see that the market clears at a lower employment level, Q_c instead of Q_2.

In other words, the surplus of labor that conventional analysis suggests exists in the face of a minimum-wage law is eliminated by the shifts in the curves. However, labor is worse off because of the wage floor and adjustments in fringe benefits. After the vertical distance between the two supply curves, ac (which, again, is labor's dollar evaluation of the fringe benefits lost because of the minimum wage) is subtracted from the

94

FIGURE 9.2 The revised view of minimum-wage laws

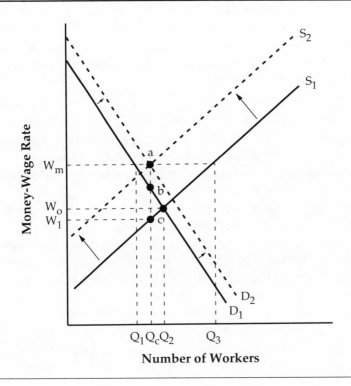

minimum wage W_m, the effective wage paid labor is reduced to W_1, or by $W_m - W_1$. In short, when labor is paid in many forms, a minimum wage reduces, not increases, the effective payment going to affected workers.

Conventional analysis suggests that a minimum wage of W_m will cause employment opportunities for labor to fall to Q_1. The adjustments that employers make to nonmoney conditions of work cause employment opportunities to fall by less, to only Q_c in Figure 9.2.[7]

Case II: Changes in Fringe Benefits
that Affect Labor Productivity

Because of the labor surplus that emerges when money wages are set at a legal minimum, employers can increase the production demands that are placed on their workers. The result can be an increase in the productivity of labor; thus, the demand curve for labor can rise. Workers who have to deal with the labor surplus must either accept the new demands placed on them or retire from the market. The supply curve contracts because of the workers' marginal evaluation of the higher production demands. The employment opportunities for labor can be expected to fall on balance because

⊃ the minimum-wage law increases the cost of labor relative to other variable resources and induces some substitution of other factors for labor, and

⊃ the law increases the overall cost of production and reduces the quantity of final product sold.

If more of other production factors are employed in lieu of labor, then a lower output can be achieved only with less labor. However, the lower employment level will, as before, be accompanied by a reduction in the effective wage going to labor.

Employers can also react to the higher wage minimum by making changes in workplace conditions, such as air conditioning, which, if reduced in use, can lower the productivity of labor.[8] Firms will make such adjustments as long as the change in the money-wage rate is greater than the dollar value of the change in labor productivity. These changes will cause the supply curve of labor to shift until it intersects the demand curve at the minimum-wage rate. The effective wage and employment opportunities are then reduced as before.

Differences in Perspective

This analysis conflicts with the conventional textbook treatment of minimum wages in several important respects. First, conventional analysis holds that the effective wage rate increases for some workers and declines for others. As noted, this is because of the implicit assumption that an increase in the minimum-wage rate is equivalent to an increase in the effective-wage rate. My analysis, however, leads to the conclusion that the effective-wage rate of *all* workers, including those who retain their jobs in spite of wage minimums, decreases; they are worse off to the extent that employers have the opportunity to adjust working conditions and fringe benefits. For that reason, minimum wages appear patently unfair to those who are covered by them (even by the standards of many of those who promote legislated wage minimums).

Second, conventional analysis predicts that the market does not clear. At any wage above competitive wage levels, there will supposedly be an "army of unemployed" equal to the difference between the quantity supplied and the quantity demanded ($Q_3 - Q_1$). From this perspective, some people who want jobs at the higher minimum will lose them. The analysis suggests that people who withdraw from work because of the minimum wage do so because they do not want their jobs at the induced lower effective-wage rate. The jobs are simply no longer worth the demands placed on some workers.

Third, standard textbook treatment of minimum-wage law suggests that measured unemployment from the imposition of wage controls should be in the range of Q_1 to Q_3. (Actual job losses should be the difference between Q_1 and Q_2.) Recognition of the various adjustments employers can make in response to any surplus of *labor* that develops leads to the conclusion that actual job losses may be quite small;[9] how small depends on the variety of adjustments that employers can make to fringe benefits (nonmoney conditions of employment) and the productivity of alternative ways of paying labor, and on the amount of time employers have to adjust to the wage law.[10] From this new perspective on the impact of minimum-wage laws, it is not at all surprising that researchers have found that minimums have decreased employment opportunities little. This is because they have had, on balance, little downward effect on the effective wage paid covered workers.

Fourth, the standard view of minimum wages assumes that unemployment arises because the number of workers willing to work expands (i.e., workers move up the market supply curve S_1). However, the exact opposite occurs in this new view: The number of workers willing to work falls (i.e., workers move down their supply curve). This is because their effective wage falls. It is also because many, but not necessarily all, of the affected workers have better alternatives in other labor markets, one of which is the market for contraband and other criminal activities.

Minimum-wage laws, in short, make many criminal activities *relatively* profitable by making money-wage deals below the mandated minimum wage illegal. Since minimum wages are likely to lead to a marginal increase in the education and experience required of prospective employees, they will tend to encourage differentially the less-advantaged workers into criminal activities.

Regardless of the initial adverse impact on employment opportunities of the covered workers, the magnitude of the effect of any *real* minimum wage should decrease with time, because over time employers will discover more ways to circumvent the laws. In addition, competitive pressures will grow, encouraging more and more employers to find ways of cutting their workers' effective wages.

Fifth, conventional analysis reveals that higher minimum wages place many people (especially those who provide a second family income

97

at the minimum wage) in higher marginal tax brackets. However, the higher tax payments only reduce the net benefit received by those who retain their jobs.

The revisions in the analysis presented here suggest that minimum wages not only throw people into higher tax brackets but also increase the money portion, and thus the taxable income portion, of their effective wage rate. This means that the *effective* marginal tax rate for people covered by the legal minimum wage is greater than specified in the tax schedules. The after-tax effective income is actually reduced by more than the drop in the effective wage rate; therefore, when the decrease in effective income is recognized, the total marginal tax rate resulting from all explicit and implicit taxes extracted from affected workers can be greater than 100 percent of the increase in money wages, which hardly seems in accord with the dictates of a progressive tax rate structure.[11]

Making Workers Worse Off: The Empirical Evidence

While still controversial, this new perspective on the adverse effects of minimum-wage laws is supported by a growing body of research.

⊃ Writing in the *American Economic Review*, Masanori Hashimoto found that under the 1967 minimum-wage hike, workers gained 32 cents in money income but lost 41 cents per hour in training—a net loss of 9 cents an hour in full-income compensation.[12]

⊃ Linda Leighton and Jacob Mincer, in one study, and Belton Fleisher, in another, came to a similar conclusion: Increases in the minimum wage reduce on-the-job training and, as a result, dampen growth in the real long-run income of covered workers.[13]

⊃ Walter Wessels found that the minimum wages caused retail establishments in New York to increase work demands. In response to a minimum-wage increase, only 714 of the surveyed stores cut back store hours, but 4,827 stores reduced the number of workers or their employees' hours worked. Thus, in most stores, fewer workers were given fewer hours to do the same work as before.[14]

⊃ The research of Belton Fleisher, William Alpert, and L. F. Dunn shows that minimum-wage increases lead to large reductions in fringe benefits and to worsening working conditions.[15]

If the minimum wage does *not* cause employers to make substantial reductions in nonmoney benefits, then increases in the minimum wage should cause (1) an increase in the labor force participation rates of covered workers (because workers would be moving up their supply curves of labor), (2) a reduction in the rate at which covered workers quit their jobs (because their jobs would then be more attractive), and (3) a significant increase in prices of production processes heavily dependent on covered minimum-wage workers. However, Wessels found little empirical support for such conclusions drawn from conventional theory. Indeed, in general, he found that minimum-wage increases had the exact opposite effect: (1) participation rates went down, (2) quit rates went up, and (3) prices did not rise appreciably—findings consistent only with the view that minimum-wage increases make workers worse off. With regard to quit rates, Wessels writes:

> I could find no industry which had a significant decrease in their quit rates. Two industries had a significant increase in their quit rates. . . . These results are only consistent with a lower full compensation. I also found that quit rates went up more in those industries with the average lowest wages, the more full compensation is reduced. I also found that in the long-run, several industries experienced a significantly large increase in the quit rate: a result only possible if minimum wages reduce full compensation.[16]

Given the findings of various studies done by Wessels and other researchers, Wessels deduced that every 10 percent increase in the hourly minimum wage will make workers 2 percent worse off.[17] This means that a $1.30 increase in the minimum (equal to the 1987 congressional proposal) could, on balance, make the covered workers worse off by 26 cents per hour.

Accordingly, a zero minimum wage, as the *Times* has recommended, would tend to raise the overall value of the compensation bundle of the targeted workers. How much depends on where the market money wage settles. A federal minimum wage of zero would not likely mean an actual money wage of zero, only that employers would not have to pay some positive wage rate. Employers would be free to lower their money-wage rate, increase their fringe benefits, and in other ways, make employment in the targeted markets more attractive. Thus, the number of low-skilled workers who would want to work in the targeted markets should be expected to rise, resulting in an increase in the actual number employed.

Notes

1. For a review of the economic literature on the minimum wage through the early 1980s, see Charles Brown, Curtis Gilroy, and Andrew Cohen, "The Effect of the Minimum Wage on Employment and Unemployment," *Journal of Economic Literature* (June 1982), pp. 487–528.
2. Indeed, profit-maximizing employers can be expected to adjust the conditions of work until the last dollar of cost incurred due to the adjustments is just equal to a dollar reduction in the money wage. Given the amount of capital employed and a competitive market, the firm's direct and indirect expenditures on labor (in a market free of government wage interference) can be expected to achieve maximum efficiency. The mathematics of the relationship between the prices of one input factor and other variable input factors is developed in C. E. Ferguson, *The Neoclassical Theory of Production and Distribution* (Cambridge University Press, 1969), chap. 6.
3. Clearly, many minimum-wage jobs do not carry standard fringe benefits, such as life and medical insurance and retirement plans. However, most do offer fringes in the form of the conditions in the work environment, attitudes of the bosses, breaks, frequency and promptness of pay, variety of work, uniforms, use of company tools and supplies, meals and drinks, and precautions against accidents. These fringes are subject to withdrawal when minimum wages are mandated.
4. More precisely, the labor markets should, after adjustments, clear more or less to the same extent as they did before the minimum-wage law was imposed. Of course, employers are not directly concerned with ensuring that their labor market clears. They are, however, interested in minimizing their labor costs, a motivation that drives them to adjust the conditions of work until the market clears. The point is that if employers are confronted by more workers than they need, they can offer less or demand more until the surplus is eliminated.
5. Remember that the demand for labor curve is the net of fringe benefits. A reduction in fringe benefits will thereby increase employer's willingness to pay higher wages, which explains the increase in (or shift outward of) the demand for labor.
6. If the vertical distance of the shift in the supply curve were not greater than the vertical distance of the shift in the demand curve, then the change in fringe benefits would have been made even in the absence of the minimum wage.
7. Indeed, if employers had an infinite number of ways to adjust non-money conditions of work, and the market money wage were a small part of total labor payment, the minimum wage would not significantly affect employment opportunities. When employers have an infinite or even a very large number of ways to pay labor, a change in the money wage by law will not significantly affect either the payment options open to employers or the ability of the employers to pay the effective market wage.
8. It should be noted that the employer must be careful in cutting back on

some fringe benefits like air conditioning, which can adversely affect higher-paid workers as well as minimum-wage workers, forcing the firm to raise the wages of those paid more than the minimum wage. However, this qualification does not affect the thrust of the argument, which is that the employer will make adjustments that are made economical by a legal wage floor.

9. Of course, dispute remains over how small is small, and empirical studies vary in their assessment of the estimated impact of the laws. James Ragan estimated that the 1972 minimum wage resulted in lost employment for approximately 320,000 teenagers. In the absence of the minimum-wage law, the youth unemployment rate would have been 3.8 percentage points lower than it was. See James F. Ragan, Jr., "Minimum Wage Legislation and the Youth Labor Market" (St. Louis, MO: Center for the Study of American Business, Washington University, 1976).

10. As indicated in note 7, if there were an infinite number of adjustments that employers could make in the nonmoney conditions of employment, then an increase in the minimum would, on the margin, have no impact on the effective wage and employment levels. In this extreme case, there would be no loss in labor productivity.

11. Finally, it should be noted that textbooks conventionally demonstrate that in monopsonistic labor markets, a minimum wage that is imposed at any level between the monopsony wage and the wage at the intersection of the marginal cost of labor curve and the demand curve for labor will result in an expansion of employment. Further, it is argued that for any employment level between the monopsony and competitive employment levels, two minimum-wage levels will result in the same level of employment. However, if the monopsonistic employer can adjust the nonmoney wage benefits of employment, then the analysis of monopsony markets needs to be revised in two respects. First, as in the competitive model, the supply of labor will tend to contract by more than the demand curve expands. An increase in the minimum wage will, therefore, result in a reduction in nonmoney wages, a decrease in the effective monopsony wage, and a decrease in the employment level. Second, a higher minimum wage will always provide employers with a greater incentive to make nonmoney wage adjustments and will lead to a greater decrease in demand for labor than a lower minimum wage. Therefore, two minimum-wage levels cannot result in the same employment levels: the higher minimum wage will always cause a greater reduction in employment opportunities than will a lower minimum wage. In summary, the employment effect of minimum wages will tend to be in the same direction in both competitive and monopsonistic labor markets.

12. Masanori Hashimoto, "Minimum Wage Effect on Training to the Job," *American Economic Review* 70 (Dec. 1982), pp. 1070–1087.

13. Linda Leighton and Jacob Mincer, "Effects of Minimum Wages on Human Capital Formation," in *The Economics of Legal Minimum Wages*," ed. Simon Rothenberg (Washington, DC: American Enterprise Institute, 1981).

14. Walter J. Wessels, "Minimum Wages: Are Workers Really Better Off?" (paper prepared for presentation at a conference on minimum wages, Washington, DC, National Chamber Foundation, July 29, 1987).
15. Belton M. Fleisher, *Minimum Wage Regulation in Retail Trade* (Washington, DC: American Enterprise Institute, 1981); William T. Alpert, "The Effects of the Minimum Wage on the Fringe Benefits of Restaurant Workers" (paper, Lehigh University, 1983); and L. F. Dunn, "Nonpecuniary Job Preferences and Welfare Losses Among Migrant Agriculture Workers," *American Journal of Agriculture Economics* 67 (May 1985), pp. 257–265.
16. Wessels, "Minimum Wages: Are Workers Really Better Off?", quote from p. 13.
17. Ibid., p. 15.

APPENDIX A

List Of Major Editorials on the Minimum Wage
Published by the *New York Times*
December 1937 to November 1993

The listing includes only editorials in which the *New York Times* editors made substantive comments on the minimum wage-and-hours provisions (but only to the hours provisions when parallels were drawn between hours and wage restrictions) of the Fair Labor Standards Act. Editorials written between 1937 and 1989 in which only passing references were made to the minimum-wage laws have not been included. Not all editorials included in this listing are cited in the body of the text.

"Wage Bill vs. Farm Labor," Dec. 9, 1937, p. 24.

* "Wages, 'North' and 'South'," Feb. 15, 1938, p. 24.

"Labor Leaders vs. Labor," May 10, 1938, p. 20.

"Scalpel—or Axe?", May 16, 1938, p. 16.

"Differentials in Wages," May 21, 1938, p. 14.

"The Question of Hours," May 22, 1938, sect. IV, p. 8.

"Legislating in the Dark," May 24, 1938, p. 18.

"House vs. Senate Version," May 25, 1938, p. 22.

"Working Hours," May 26, 1938, p. 24.

"Minimum Wages and NRA," May 27, 1938, p. 16.

"The Wage Bill Compromise," June 2, 1938, p. 22.

"'Standard Procedure,'" June 3, 1938, p. 20.

* "The Verdict of Economists," June 4, 1938, p. 14.

"The Method of Reform," June 5, 1938, sect. IV, p. 8.

"'Principle' vs. Substance," June 8, 1938, p. 22.

"The Final Wage–Hour Bill," June 14, 1938, p. 20.

"A Potential Joker," June 16, 1938, p. 22.

"'No. 1 Economic Problem,'" July 7, 1938, p. 18.

* "Wage–Hour Law Effects," Nov. 12, 1938, p. 14.

"Interpreting the Wage Act," Aug. 16, 1938, p. 18.

"A Revised Wage–Hour Act," Apr. 27, 1939, p. 24.

---

*The full text of these editorials has been included in Appendix B.

"A New Dispute in Congress," July 21, 1939, p. 18.
"Mr. Andrews Changes His Mind," July 22, 1939, p. 14.
"Andrews Out, Fleming In," Oct. 19, 1939, p. 22.
"The Wage–Hour Act," Oct. 23, 1939, p. 18.
"Amending the Wage–Hour Law," Apr. 12, 1940, p. 22.
"Wage–Hour Amendments," Apr. 25, 1940, p. 22.
"Wage–Hour Amendments," Apr. 29, 1940, p. 14.
"Time for Responsibility," May 6, 1940, p. 16.
"Wage–Hour Act Revision," Apr. 5, 1941, p. 16.
"Wage–Hour Interpretation," June 12, 1942, p. 20.
"The Forty-Hour Week," June 14, 1942, sect. IV, p. 10.
"Wages and Families," May 6, 1943, p. 18.
"'Mandatory' Wage Increases," Sept. 1, 1943, p. 18.
"Post-War Guarantees," Dec. 3, 1944, sect. IV, p. 8.
"Price Controls: War and Peace," Apr. 9, 1945, p. 18.
"Wage Policy," July 24, 1945, p. 22.
"The President's Message," Sept. 7, 1945, p. 22.
"Minimum Wages," Mar. 27, 1946, p. 26.
"Wage Facts and Theories," Apr. 13, 1946, p. 16.
"New Minimum Wage," Jan. 28, 1950, p. 26.
"Mr. Mitchell's Good Start," Nov. 19, 1953, p. 30.
"Farm Props vs. Wage Floors," May 5, 1955, p. 32.
* "Raising the Minimum Wage," June 14, 1955, p. 28.
"New Floor for Wages," Mar. 1, 1956, p. 32.
"State Minimum Wages," Mar. 12, 1956, p. 26.
"Supports and Soapboxes," Apr. 14, 1956, p. 16.
"Wage Floor Extensions," May 14, 1956, p. 24.
"Wage Floor Extensions," Feb. 28, 1957, p. 26.
"Low Wages in New York," Sept. 26, 1959, p. 22.
"State Wage Law Proposals," Nov. 19, 1959, p. 38.
* "The City Council and Wages," Dec. 19, 1959, p. 26.
"Low Wages and Relief," Feb. 22, 1960, p. 16.
"New Minimum Wage," Jan. 26, 1960, p. 26.
"Minimum Wage Law Revision," Feb. 9, 1961, p. 30.
"Minimum Wage, 1961," Mar. 21, 1961, p. 36.
"President and Congress," Mar. 29, 1961, p. 22.
"Minimum Wage in the Senate," Apr. 13, 1961, p. 34.
* "The Minimum Wage," Apr. 23, 1961, sect. IV, p. 12.
"Minimum Wage Compromise," May 2, 1961, p. 36.
"A Dollar and Up an Hour," Sept. 5, 1961, p. 34.
"A Municipal Wage Floor," Jan. 1, 1962, p. 22.

APPENDIX A: LIST OF EDITORIALS ON MINIMUM WAGE

* "A Municipal Wage Floor," Aug. 13, 1962, p. 24.
"Falling Through the Wage Floor," Aug. 20, 1962, p. 22.
"New York Can't Live Alone," Sept. 18, 1962, p. 38.
"The City's Wage Experiment," Oct. 25, 1962, p. 38.
"Wrong Wage Solution," June 25, 1964, p. 32.
"Unconstitutional Wage Floor," Aug. 26, 1964, p. 38.
* "Wrong Way on Wages," Mar. 24, 1965, p. 42.
"Floor Under Farm Wages," Aug. 5, 1965, p. 28.
"Beating the Minimums," Sept. 3, 1965, p. 26.
"Fight Over the Union Shop," May 19, 1965, p. 46.
"Inescapable Veto," Apr. 19, 1965, p. 28.
* "An Up-From-Poverty Wage," Feb. 22, 1966, p. 22.
"Raising the Wage Floor," Mar. 14, 1966, p. 30.
"Retreat on Minimum Wage," May 26, 1966, p. 46.
"Aiding the Working Poor," Aug. 23, 1966, p. 38.
"Higher Wage Floor," Sept. 2, 1966, p. 30.
"Raising the Wage Floor," Sept. 17, 1966, p. 28.
"The Liberal Party's Role," Feb. 1, 1969, p. 28.
* "The City Council as Canute," Oct. 13, 1969, p. 44.
"Two Billion for Poverty and $1.85 for Working Poor,"
       Jan. 7, 1970, p. 42.
"Reforming Welfare, and a Wage–Welfare Interlock,"
       Apr. 26, 1971, p. 34.
"Sensible Minimum," May 12, 1972, p. 40.
"Wider Wage Floor," June 24, 1972, p. 30.
"The Last Month," Sept. 18, 1972, p. 24.
* "'Let Them Eat Cake,'" Oct. 5, 1972, p. 46.
"Snug Harbor for Protectionists," Oct. 23, 1971, p. 32.
"Floor Under Wages," Apr. 11, 1973, p. 46.
"Congress Fights Back," Aug. 5, 1973, sect. IV, p. 14.
"Low-End Justice," Aug. 28, 1973, p. 34.
"Wrong-End Squeeze," Sept. 7, 1973, p. 34.
"Minimum Wage Fiasco," Sept. 20, 1973, p. 46.
"Ceiling Unlimited," Sept. 22, 1973, p. 30.
"Unzippered Pocketbook," Oct. 6, 1973, p. 22.
"Political Reversal, Congress Fumbles," Dec. 23, 1973, sect. IV, p. 10
"Sub-Minimum," Feb. 9, 1974, p. 28.
"Higher Pay Floor," Mar. 2, 1974, p. 30.
"Lagging Minimum," Mar. 24, 1974, sect. IV, p. 16.
"Bottom Up," Apr. 12, 1974, p. 30.
"More Work," Feb. 7, 1976, p. 20.

* "The Minimally Useful Minimum Wage," Mar. 21, 1977, p. 26.
"Labor Loses Two in a Row," Mar. 26, 1977, p. 18.
* "The Cruel Cost of the Minimum Wage," Aug. 17, 1977, p. 20.
"Paying Fairer Dues in the South," Aug. 20, 1977, p. 20.
"The Minimum Wage, Continued," Aug. 29, 1977, p. 26.
"Reprise," Sept. 20, 1977, p. 40.
"Minimum Reform for Minimum Wages," Dec. 22, 1978, p. 32.
"Tinkering with the Minimum Wage," Dec. 2, 1980, p. A18.
"Job Opportunities—for Children," July 22, 1982, p. 22.
"Making Haste to Make Few Jobs," Mar. 14, 1983, sect. I, p. 14.
"Why Pay Less to Teen-agers?", Mar. 21, 1985, sect. I, p. 30.
* "The Right Minimum Wage: $0.00," Jan. 14, 1987, p. 18.
"Look: Liberalism!", Jan. 15, 1987, sect. IV, p. 20.
* "Don't Raise the Minimum Wage," Apr. 15, 1987, p. 20.
"The Minimum-Wage Illusion," Feb. 23, 1988, p. 24.
"Better than $3.35, $4.25 or Even $5.05," July 11, 1988, sect. I, p. 16.
"The Minimum Wage: A Better Way," Sept. 21, 1988, sect. I, p. 22.
"The Minimum Wage: A Detraction," Mar. 22, 1989, sect. I, p. 26.
"A Veto That Can Help the Poor," June 15, 1989, sect. I, p. 30.
"Help, at Last, for the Working Poor," Nov. 2, 1989, p. 20.
"Don't Sacrifice the Needy Workers," June 7, 1993, p. A14.

APPENDIX B

Selected Editorials on the Minimum Wage
Published by the *New York Times*
between February 1938 and November 1989

"Wages, 'North' and 'South'"
(Feb. 15, 1938, p. 24)

One of the most important criticisms that have been made of the proposed Federal Wage and Hour Bill is that, if it attempted to establish a flat minimum wage for the whole country it would in effect act as a tariff wall in the North against Southern goods. It might make it so difficult for Southern employers to compete that many of them would be forced to close down. Both directly and indirectly it might increase unemployment in the South. Those workers in the South who retained their jobs and did get more because of a Federal wage law would be in a more precarious position. To meet this criticism, it has been suggested that a differential be established between the minimum wages set for the North and those set for the South. The President is reported to have suggested that this differential be set at $2 a week—that a minimum wage of $13 be prescribed for the North and of $11 for the South.

Such a solution fails to recognize the real complexity of the problem. Any minimum wage law would be unsettling if the legal differential it established between one section and another was either substantially greater or substantially less than that brought about by competitive conditions. If the differential were too small, it would work against the Southern employer; if it were too large, it would work against the Northern employer. An excessive legal differential would be particularly ironic, for it would penalize the section and the employers that had already been paying the higher wages.

Brief examination of the problem, moreover, is not enough to show that it could not be solved by adopting "a" differential between the "North" and the "South," but only by adopting a highly complicated network of differentials as between sections, States, towns, and industries. "North" and "South," for example, though convenient short-hand terms, are not two separate entities with uniform conditions within themselves. A recent study based on an analysis of the census of manufacturers for 1929 showed that the average cost of labor per man-hour in manufacturing in that year was 23 cents in South Carolina, 36 cents in Virginia, 40 cents in Maine, and 61 cents in Wyoming. There was a far greater difference, in other words, between the latter and the Northern State of Maine. There were thirty differentials rather than one.

The real complexity of the problem is indicated by a recent study by the National Industrial Conference Board of conditions in September of last year. The wage differential existing between one section and another varies with each industry. The board divided the country into the "East," the "South," the "Middle West" and the "Far West." In the furniture industry, it found that the hourly earnings of male workers averaged 42.2 cents in the South, and in the Far West 63.7 cents, a difference of 50.9 per cent. In the lumber industry, however, it found that hourly earnings, in the South averaged 32.7 cents, and in the Far West 74.9 cents, a differential of 129.1 per cent.

It was found that there were also great differences in wages depending on the size of cities in which plants were located. Combining the five industries that the board studied, it was found that the difference in average hourly earnings between the group of cities having a population over 500,000 and the group with less than 10,000 inhabitants was 43.2 per cent. There were also great differences between wages in each industry. For the country as a whole, wages in the cotton industry, for example, were 46 cents an hour and wages in the printing industry 95 cents an hour.

It is also interesting to notice that the wage differential between the South and the rest of the country is much greater than the calculated differences in the cost of living. The cost of living in the South is placed at 96.5 per cent of that of the country as a whole, while the hourly wages paid in the cotton textile industry were only 92.6 per cent as high, in machine shops only 86.8 per cent as high, in furniture only 77.7 per cent as high, and in lumber only 61.1 per cent as high.

These complexities point to the dilemma of a Federal Wage–Hour Bill. If it disregards the differentials in wages as between actions, States, large and small towns and different industries, and attempts to impose a single minimum, it must create profound disturbances. If the effort is made to write differentials into the bill, they must be extremely numerous and complex; there is no guarantee that they will be "right," and even if they should be "right" at the beginning, changes in conditions—in price levels, in particular industries, or in particular sections—would soon make them wrong. If the attempt is made to escape this horn of the dilemma by allowing some commission or administrator to fix differentials at its discretion, then we create the arbitrariness and the day-to-day uncertainties of delegated power.

The wisest solution is to leave minimum wage laws to the individual

States. Half of them have already adopted such legislation, mainly within the last five years.

"The Verdict of Economists"
(June 4, 1938, p. 14)

It might pay some of the advocates of the widespread doctrine that ever and ever higher wage rates are a sure recipe for recovery to learn what some of the best economists have written on the subject. One of the facts that economists have discovered over and over again is that when a commodity or a service is forced by law, monopoly or other conditions above the "equilibrium" price that free competition would tend to establish, a certain portion of it remains unsold. Some commodities, like salt and pepper, have what economists call an "inelastic" demand. They are needed in certain amounts, but no more; they are unimportant factors in the individual's budget, and a raising or lowering of the price within wide limits hardly affects the quantity consumed. But other commodities, like automobiles and radios, have a highly "elastic" demand. A small raising of the price may greatly contract, or a small lowering of the price may greatly increase, the quantity sold.

Just how elastic is the demand for the services of workers? In recent years two prominent economists, working independently, have undertaken to answer this question with as much precision as possible, and have arrived at almost identical results. One of these is Professor Paul H. Douglas of the University of Chicago. The other is Professor A. C. Pigou of Cambridge University. Working from an enormous range of statistical data, Professor Douglas arrived at the following conclusion (pp. 501–502, "The Theory of Wages," 1934):

> The fact that the elasticity of the demand for labor seems to be between -3.0 and -4.0 indicates that where unemployment is caused by a wage rate which is higher than marginal productivity, a reduction of 1 per cent in the rate of wages should normally lead to an increase of 3 or 4 per cent in the volume of employment and hence to an increase in the total income of the workers of from 2 to 3 per cent. If wages are pushed up above the point of marginal productivity, the decrease in employment would normally be from three to four times as great as the increase in hourly rates, so that the total income of the working class would be reduced in the ratio indicated above. It should also be noted that Pigou in his recent "Theory of Unemployment" arrives by almost purely deductive methods

at an almost identical estimate of the elasticity of demand for labor during periods of depression, namely, that it is "probably not less than -3.0" [Pigou, p. 97].

It does not follow, however, that the cause of unemployment is uniformly a wage which is in excess of marginal productivity. There are other causes of seasonal, cyclical, and technological nature and in these cases a reduction in the wage rate need not invariably bring the greater expansion in employment.

There may be some disagreement regarding whether the precise ratio arrived at by Professors Douglas and Pigou has been established. But they do make a very impressive case for their contention that a 1 per cent change in the wage rate can make at least a 3 per cent change in the volume of employment. If the ratio should be somewhat less than this, it is still clear that arbitrary raising of wage rates above the productivity level is definitely adverse to the interests of labor and to the general welfare. It is to the interests of all that labor should get its full economic wage, but it is to the interests of no one, labor least of all, that an unduly high hourly rate should breed heavy unemployment.

"Wage–Hour Law Effects"
(Nov. 12, 1938, p. 14)

Commissioner Andrew's report on the unemployment caused by the Federal Wage–Hour Law is candid in its presentation of fact, but strange in its reasoning. Mr. Andrews tells us that not more than 30,000 to 50,000 persons have so far been laid off as a result of the act, and that most of these were in the pecan shelling, tobacco stemming, lumber and bagging industries. His estimate may or may not be accurate, but it is undoubtedly honest. Yet he goes on to offer some odd reasons why these figures should not be taken too seriously:

> The significance of the lay-offs is . . . reduced by the fact that a large share of the total consists of marginal and handicapped workers, whose position in the economic system has long been insecure.

In other words, the significance of the lay-offs is reduced by the fact that the persons affected are those who were already among the worst off! But it was precisely these marginal and handicapped workers that the act was designed to help. And it was precisely these persons that critics of the measure, before its passage, predicted would be adversely affected. It is no satisfaction to these workers to learn from Mr. Andrew's report that some of them "are already being replaced by more efficient workers able to earn the minimum hourly rate." Such replacement, moreover, can occur only in a period when there is already a large reservoir of unemployment to draw from.

The Commissioner's report is none the less an important step toward a realistic attitude toward the Wage–Hour Act. Speaking of the shutdowns in the pecan industry, he writes: "Both employers and leaders of the employees contend that the minimum wage rate cannot be paid immediately." If the Federal act had been modeled on the better State minimum wage laws the present dilemma would not exist. Most of the States have not been foolish enough to write definite minima into their laws; a fact-finding body would first determine by investigation what minimum wage an industry could immediately stand and it would be fixed no higher than that.

It does not help the former pecan workers and others to be told that their previous wages were "notoriously low" anyhow. They already knew that. But the point overlooked by so many reformers is that, low as those wages were, they must have appeared to the marginal workers themselves to offer the best alternative open to them. The question now is, are the workers who have been dropped better or worse off than they were before? They will doubtless be put on relief, when they can prove that their resources are exhausted. But some of them may find their situation ironic. The Government tells them, in effect, that for a forty-four-hour week they must not be offered and cannot accept less than $47 a month. Because they cannot earn quite this amount they are thrown on relief. The States in which most of them have been laid off are Texas, Georgia and North Carolina. This Summer persons on general relief in Texas were getting an average of $9 a month, in Georgia of $6, in North Carolina of $5.50.

Minimum wage laws, within certain modest limits, can be helpful; pushed beyond those limits they can do more harm than good. Perhaps in time we will begin to learn that we cannot raise ourselves indefinitely by our economic bootstraps; and that our social legislation must be judged, not merely by the nobility of the moral sentiments that inspired it, but by its actual economic consequences.

"Raising the Minimum Wage"
(June 14, 1955, p. 28)

The Senate bill to raise the federal minimum wage from 75 cents to $1 represents a compromise between two forces of great political power. On the one side are the President and his Administration team who have recommended 90 cents; on the other is a formidable array of labor's cohorts who have urged that the floor be upped to $1.25.

The Administration argues that a 90-cent level would do a little better than keep up with the cost of living. However, it fears that any higher lift would be hard for employers to absorb—resulting in business failures and unemployment.

In addition to the cost-of-living argument, points in labor's brief have been that the minimum wage has failed to keep pace with general wage increases, that at least $1.25 is needed to maintain an adequate living standard and that experience has proved industries can take care of the proposed increase—especially as labor's productivity has gone up 20 per cent since the previous boost was made. On still another point which labor makes some Northern employers have openly agreed: that a substantial increase will reduce "unfair" regional competition based on lower wage costs in the South.

While the Senate bill is a compromise between labor and Administration views it ignores a demand which both groups have made—wider coverage. The Administration hasn't been specific, but labor urges extending the act to cover workers in local operations of firms doing an interstate business. Also ignored has been opposition to any change, spearheaded by the National Association of Manufacturers.

This whole matter is now before the House. We believe a substantial increase in the minimum wage and widened coverage are badly needed and we urge the House to recognize that need. How much of a change should be made should depend on the best informed estimate of how far the additional costs can successfully be absorbed by industry through increasing productivity and expanding operations.

On this point two impartial sets of data offer useful evidence. The United States Department of Labor thoroughly studied the effects of the previous increase made in 1950 from 40 to 75 cents—35 cents compared with 25 cents in the Senate bill and the 50 cents which labor wants. This showed that the 1950 raise had no marked effect either on employment or business mortality—in spite of the dire predictions of opponents of the change. Also the census figures show that in the South, where the burden of the raise must have fallen heaviest, gains in almost every industry in the past six years have exceeded those of relatively high-wage New England.

"The City Council and Wages"
(Dec. 19, 1959, p. 26)

The New York City Council is not the body to pass minimum wage legislation. But it could make a useful contribution to an understanding of the need for such a law in this city and what its effect would be.

Mayor Wagner, it is reported, will ask Councilman Earl Brown to introduce a resolution urging the State Legislature and Congress to impose a floor on wages of $1.25 an hour. The usefulness of such a resolution would depend entirely on the amount, and the validity, of the information which would be furnished to the public, now badly in need of enlightenment.

The necessity for a minimum wage law here, of course, is directly related to the adequacy of wages now being paid to workers in New York. In some industries, such as construction, printing and longshore operations, scales compare favorably with those in other cities. But the pay of factory workers, largely Puerto Ricans and Negroes, is shockingly low—next to the lowest in the twenty cities with a factory population of more than 100,000. All this is known in a general way, but detailed wage comparisons and trends, with estimates of the adequacy of wages and explanations of the low ones, have not been made nor widely publicized, as they certainly ought to be.

Then, too, there are the questions as to what the effect of a minimum wage, say of $1.25, would be. For example, how many of those now employed would be affected? How much of a financial burden would such a measure impose on business and what would be its effects on industrial migration? Also, how much less of a burden would there be on the city's taxpayers because of lessened cost of public welfare and relief?

The suggested Brown resolution would call for public hearings to give employers, unions and civic agencies a chance to give their views about a $1.25 minimum wage. The need is far greater for a study by an impartial agency, skilled in public and business administration, which would assemble and appraise the facts as to the leading questions involved. The Council ought to provide for such a study first and hold the hearings after the findings are known—and made widely so.

"The Minimum Wage"
(Apr. 23, 1961, sect. IV, p. 12)

Now that the Senate and the House have passed bills extending minimum-wage coverage to workers in the retail, service and construction industries—but with widely differing provisions—there is little doubt that some such measure will get final approval by Congress. We think the Senate bill is the better of the two.

The basic $1.25 minimum of the Senate measure (contrasted with $1.15 in the House bill) is justified by both the need and the probable effects. Time is allowed for the necessary adjustments by employers—that is, the largest concerns best able to meet the additional costs.

Experience with previous minimum-wage bills has shown that opponents' fears of business calamity and increased unemployment were much exaggerated. Certainly workers getting less than the $50 for a forty-hour week which the Senate measure would guarantee need at least that much for a decent family existence, and business recovery would be helped if they should get it.

Furthermore, we believe that the minimum should be as widely applied as possible within the interstate commerce limits set by the Constitution. The Senate bill's coverage of about 4,000,000 additional persons is far more to be desired than the 1,200,000 coverage of the House measure, especially as the exceptions in the latter are much wider than necessary to exempt firms engaged in purely intrastate commerce. The exemptions in the Senate bill of concerns making purchases of less than $250,000 a year across state lines would accomplish that.

The Senate–House conferees should accept the Senate's basic standards both as to the amount of the minimum and also the coverage involved. Room for the compromises necessary to reach an agreement lies in special exemptions which would have but a minor effect. But the closer the conferees' report will be to the Senate bill the better it will be.

"A Municipal Wage Floor"
(Aug. 13, 1962, p. 24)

The shockingly low wages earned by many workers in this city have long been a community disgrace. Now Mayor Wagner is under intense labor pressure to eliminate such wages through a municipal law establishing a minimum wage of $1.50 an hour for all workers in the five boroughs. The only thing wrong with this "remedy" is that it would eliminate jobs as well as low wages.

New York is not an economic island, immune from the competition of other cities and states. Its principal industry, the apparel trades, lost 70,000 manufacturing jobs in the last decade. The bulk went to communities elsewhere in this state, Pennsylvania, New Jersey and the South, where employers felt labor costs would be lower. this trend would be vastly accelerated if New York pushed its statutory wage floor far above Federal or state standards.

The national minimum wage now stands at $1.15 an hour and is scheduled to rise to $1.25 in September of next year. The state minimum will increase from $1 to $1.15 on Oct. 15 of this year and will go to $1.25 two years after that. No legislative fiat can compel employers with little capital investment and limited need for highly skilled labor to stay in New York if it pushes its minimum so much above those prevailing elsewhere. The chief sufferers would be the very Negro and Puerto Rican workers in the unskilled and semi-unskilled categories for whom the law is intended to provide primary benefit.

A more realistic approach would be the creation of industry-by-industry wage boards to recommend higher minimums where the result would be higher income and not job abolition. Obviously, many service and entertainment industries depend so completely on the rich New York market that they could not uproot themselves in search of cheap labor.

But even this will provide no adequate answer to the problem of industrial slum clearance. If we are to rid ourselves of the heavy toll low wages exact in supplemental relief payments, ill health and squalor, the city will have to work hard to attract better-paying industries through participation in the state's new industrial development fund and other measures to improve the business climate here. Our representatives in Washington and Albany will have to strive more energetically for higher Federal and state minimums to guard against the pirating of New York jobs. The danger of an artificial rush to the front of the parade lies in making New York's economy more vulnerable to the predatory tactics of those who want to steal our industries and turn more of our workers into public charges.

"Wrong Way on Wages"
(Mar. 24, 1965, p. 42)

The head of a family in the United States of 1965 should not have to get along on a wage of less than $1.50 an hour. But the method the Democratic majority at Albany has devised to establish such a wage floor for workers in New York State is likely to generate at least as much misery as it relieves.

By proposing to raise the statutory minimum wage in New York to $1.50 an hour, 25 cents above the national level, the Democrats encourage an accelerated flight to New Jersey, Pennsylvania and the South of garment factories and other light manufacturing industries. Negroes and Puerto Ricans, who make up much of the work force in these industries, will thus have the assurance of higher wages—but no jobs to earn them in.

The impact of a higher general minimum is also likely to be a reduced disposition by employers to hire youngsters entering the job market, the group already most heavily afflicted by unemployment. For out-of-school teen-agers the idleness rate is now more than triple that for other workers.

There are two things both parties in New York ought to be doing in the minimum wage field that make more sense than treating this state as an economic island. One is to concentrate on the demand for a higher Federal minimum, to which a general increase in the New York pay floor would be linked. The other is to press for more tripartite industry wage-boards, to consider the setting of higher rates in those industries that are not directly affected by out-of-state competition and that do have the capacity to pay more without curtailing employment or forcing enter-prises into bankruptcy.

"An Up-From-Poverty Wage"
(Feb. 22, 1966, p. 22)

The Fair Labor Standards Act has been revised several times since its original passage in 1938, but it still covers only about half of the workers who are employed for a wage or salary. Now dormant in the House of Representatives is a bill to increase the present minimum wage from $1.25 an hour to $1.75 over a period of years and to extend the law's coverage to eight million additional workers.

The Democratic leaders in the House are not pushing the bill, be-cause their private count suggests that they could not beat off crippling amendments to the bill in its present form. There is also dissension within the Administration on the issue. Although Secretary of Labor Wirtz joins organized labor in strongly supporting a higher minimum, the Council of Economic Advisers fears that too sharp an increase may spur inflation.

The council's concern does not center on the lowest-paid workers, who would be immediately affected and whose claim to an increase is undeniably just, but rather on other workers all the way up the pay scale who would clamor for fresh increases to maintain their relative advantage. Their demands would not necessarily be just but they would be hard to resist and would be inflationary.

Some economists argue that a higher minimum wage and wider coverage tend to squeeze out marginal firms and to speed up the move toward automation wherever feasible. These adverse effects hit hardest at the unskilled workers and the teen-agers looking for work, two groups the Government is trying to help. However, these side effects would be diminished if trade unions relaxed their opposition to indirect Government subsidies to marginal firms in the form of training grants and other help for their employees.

Sentiment on Capitol Hill appears to be moving toward a sensible compromise that would raise the minimum in two stages, first to $1.40 and then to $1.60. Such an increase would bring help to the low-paid workers who imperatively need it without setting off a sharp wage rise all along the line. In any event, the conflict over the exact size of the increase should not obscure the necessity for extending coverage, particularly to the long-exploited agricultural laborers. It is a disgrace that many thousands of full-time workers still earn wages so low they require public relief payments to feed and house their families.

"The City Council as Canute"
(Oct. 13, 1969, p. 44)

Almost a thousand years have passed since King Canute tried, and failed, to order the tides. That same quixotic spirit has re-emerged in the City Council's attempt to control the economic tides, at least as they relate to minimum wages. Against Mayor Lindsay's advice, the Council unanimously voted to require that all suppliers to the city must pay at least $2.50 an hour, a figure more than 50 per cent above the national minimum wage rate of $1.60 an hour.

Legend has it that King Canute knew the tides would not obey his will and issued his edict mainly to show his courtiers he did not have divine powers. But the City Council seems to take its decree to be a "pacesetter" for the nation. This ignores the fact that even New York City's large budget is only a small fraction of the national income, so that many suppliers will simply find it more profitable to avoid selling to the city than to meet this requirement. Even that development will result only if a serious effort is made to enforce the order, which seems doubtful. Is the city really going to check the wages of every company that sells it gasoline, coffee, light bulbs, pillow cases and a million and one other commodities?

There is a more serious objection than impracticality to the City Council move. Such an excessive minimum wage actually tends to hurt those the Councilmen seek to help; the unskilled, the handicapped, the young. There are many such people whose services are simply not worth $2.50 an hour. They will not be employed if that is the minimum wage, though they might be employable at a lower rate. New York City enterprises are in competition with many low-pay areas throughout the country, so any effort really to enforce a $2.50 minimum would increase pressures for business to leave the city. Even though it is only a few weeks before election, we trust Mayor Lindsay will have the courage to veto this bill.

"'Let Them Eat Cake'"
(Oct. 5 1972, p. 46)

Marie Antoinette seems to have taken over as dictator of policy on Capitol Hill. The 92d Congress, rushing toward adjournment, is busily slamming doors on the needs of the nation's poorest citizens, both those on welfare and those working for sweatshop wages.

The Senate has now voted to kill any prospect of genuine welfare reform for at least five years by authorizing a series of pointless tests aimed at sweeping the whole politically irksome problem under the rug while eleven million mothers and children languish in a degrading and ruinously expensive welfare system.

In the House a deadlock between conservatives and liberals appears likely to rule out any change in the Federal minimum wage of $1.60 an hour, even though both House and Senate decided months ago that some increase was essential to offset a rise of nearly one-quarter in living costs since the last boost in February 1968.

It is inconceivable that a Congress in which leaders of both parties have vied with one another and with President Nixon in proclaiming their devotion to the work ethic should end with such an outrageous injustice to the working poor. No vast skills at collective bargaining should be required to effect a compromise between the feuding House factions on just what can be agreed upon in conference with the Senate.

In our judgment, a sound compromise—one that would balance the need for offsetting inflation's bite against the danger of triggering more inflation or killing job opportunities—would couple the step-two pay increase provided by the House with the broadened coverage approved by the Senate. In any event, Congressmen cannot in conscience go home telling millions of workers at the bottom of the wage ladder that there ought to be a higher floor under the ladder—but that there won't be because the House could not trust its own conferees to reach a compromise with the Senate.

Unfortunately, the miserable botch the Senate and the Administration have made of the once promising drive toward welfare reform provides little basis for optimism that decency will prevail on facing up to the needs of the working poor. The President's refusal to back the

Ribicoff compromise on putting a Federal floor under family income doomed the imaginative proposal Mr. Nixon himself had initiated in 1969.

By the time the Senate got around this week to voting on an odd bag of proposals to reform and deform welfare, the Nixon plan had become a political orphan everyone was eager to bury. Secretary Richardson of Education and Welfare must have known how futile it was to send the Senators a last-minute warning that the time-wasting tests they approved yesterday would have results tragic for those on welfare and for the nation. After all, it was Secretary Richardson's relief aides who joined with Senator Ribicoff in hammering out the compromises which the President disowned. Its death meant death for reform.

"The Minimally Useful Minimum Wage"
(Mar. 21, 1977, p. 26)

Congress will debate a new minimum wage this spring, but this time there's a twist. Organized labor, drained by the battle to raise the wage floor every few years, is pushing for a permanent solution: indexing. This approach, proposed by John Dent, chairman of the House Labor Standards Subcommittee, would replace the current $2.30 minimum with an index keyed to the average manufacturing wage. Chairman Dent wants the minimum set at 55 percent of that average wage—about $2.85 an hour this year—and 60 percent in 1978 about $3.30. With such an index, the minimum wage would automatically be tied to the fortunes of industrial workers, eliminating the need for periodic Congressional amendments.

Since the Depression, liberals have favored higher minimum wages while conservatives have resisted. But this debate has become sterile. Whatever the merits of minimum wages in the past, they make little economic sense today, whether determined by indexing or in the old-fashioned way.

Organized labor favors a high minimum wage because that reduces management's resistance to union recruiting. Where cheap alternative sources of labor are eliminated, high-priced union labor no longer looks so bad to company managers. Support for a wage floor also comes from people with generous hearts. Is it fair, they ask, to require anyone to work for $70 or $80 a week, the take-home pay of employees earning the $2.30 minimum?

It may not be fair, but a higher minimum offers no remedy. Some businesses that pay low wages respond to an increased wage floor with or without an index—by cutting back operations or switching to labor-saving techniques. According to the Department of Labor, eight million

119

workers would be directly affected by the $2.85 minimum. A majority would probably benefit from higher paychecks. But some workers would be laid off or forced into the fringe of the labor market not covered by the minimum wage laws. Just how many jobs would disappear is not known: rough calculations put the figure between 200,000 and one million.

Snowbelt representatives, eager to staunch the flow of industry to the South, offer an additional rationale for minimum wages. They argue that urban living costs and union pressure force companies in older cities to pay high wages, even without a minimum wage. Thus a substantial boost in the minimum would fall most heavily on the low-wage states, and make them less of a lure to corporations in the North.

A higher floor would indeed make Northern cities more competitive with small towns in Mississippi. But a hitch remains: some poor people would benefit at the expense of other poor people. And if a higher minimum wage did shift more unskilled jobs to the Snowbelt, would anyone up North really want the result—more unemployed people in Mississippi with no choice but to head for those jobs in Detroit?

Some proponents of higher minimum wages suggest a compromise: to raise the minimum for adults, but to exempt teen-agers, the group that is most vulnerable to layoffs. The idea has a certain appeal. Young workers need the extra money less than the typical adult, who must support a family. Exempting teen-agers, however, would induce employers to sub-stitute cheaper young labor for more expensive adult labor, a substitution of dubious social benefit. The idea looks particularly bad after the discov-ery by Edward Gramlich, a Michigan economist, that many teen-age workers are members of middle-class families, not the intended benefici-aries of a lower youth minimum.

A higher minimum wage is no answer to poverty, and the indexing gimmick can't work any better to improve the lot of the neediest citizens.

"The Cruel Cost of the Minimum Wage"
(Aug. 17, 1977, p. 20)

The Democratic Congressional leadership and the President are strug-gling to design effective job programs. How then can they support new minimum wage legislation that will make it more difficult for unskilled workers to find employment on their own?

Next month the House will vote on an Administration-backed plan to raise the minimum wage from $2.30 to $2.65 an hour, with a provision to maintain it in the future at 53 percent of average manufacturing wages. The plan is a compromise, adopted in the face of strong opposition from the President's economic advisers; organized labor pushed hard for $3.00. Even at $2.65, though, most economists expect that the new minimum will cost jobs. Those affected will be workers on the lowest rung of the employment ladder—the very young and old, minorities, and the handicapped.

A higher minimum wage, to many, is a simple matter of economic justice. People who work hard 40 hours a week deserve their share of the good life. Yet a full-time job at the prevailing $2.30 minimum—$4,600 a year—hardly pays for food and shelter, let alone first-run movies or weekend barbecues. The working poor could indeed use more than they now earn. But to raise incomes by raising the minimum wage means that some would lose their chance to work altogether.

A business hires workers only if their labor produces earnings at least equal to their wages. If the business is compelled to pay $2.65, it cannot hire those whose work produces less than that. So although a $2.65 minimum would improve the lot of many who work below that wage today, it would at the same time destroy the jobs of those at the very bottom. Any increase in the minimum wage would be a mistake.

Even those who favor raising the minimum wage are having second thoughts about its impact on teen-agers. Unemployment among the young seeking their first jobs already hovers around 20 percent; black teen-ager unemployment is probably closer to 40 percent. A hike to a $2.65 minimum could eliminate jobs for about 100,000 of the five million 16-to-19-year-olds now in the labor force.

These doleful statistics have led a number of House members to propose exemptions for teen-agers. Illinois Republican John Erlenborn's amendment to set the wage floor for teen-agers at 75 percent of the adult minimum was narrowly defeated in the House Education and Labor Committee. Proponents are expected to try again when the House debates the minimum wage bill next month.

If there must be any increase in the minimum wage at all, at first glance, some form of youth differential does seem attractive. As a group, teen-agers are most adversely affected by minimum wages because a high percentage of them have no skills or experience. But on closer examination, there is no compelling case for a special break for teen-agers. It is individuals, finally, not groups, who suffer from unemployment. A 40-year-old textile worker with a family has just as much right to a job as a 17-year-old high school dropout. There is no justification for Congress to give employers incentives to hire the young at the expense of others.

Michigan economist Edward Gramlich's research provides another argument against treating young workers differently. A large proportion of poorly paid, unskilled teen-age workers come from middle-income homes. Fully 40 percent live with families whose incomes exceed $15,000 per year. Thus a minimum-wage exemption designed to aid Harlem teen-agers is as likely to provide jobs for suburban 18-year-olds. And they may displace adult workers who support families.

The basic effect of an increase in the minimum wage, then, would be to intensify the cruel competition among the poor for scarce jobs. If we are serious about insuring a decent income for those willing to work, let us do so directly by creating jobs through government programs and subsidizing the labor of those who are unproductive. Minimum-wage legislation has no place in a strategy to eliminate poverty.

"The Right Minimum Wage: $0.00"
(Jan. 14, 1987, p. 18)

The Federal minimum wage has been frozen at $3.35 an hour for six years. In some states, it now compares unfavorably even with welfare benefits available without working. It's no wonder then that Edward Kennedy, the new chairman of the Senate Labor Committee, is being pressed by organized labor to battle for an increase.

No wonder, but still a mistake. Anyone working in America surely deserves a better living standard than can be managed on $3.35 an hour. But there's a virtual consensus among economists that the minimum wage is an idea whose time has passed. Raising the minimum wage by a substantial amount would price working poor people out of the job market. A far better way to help them would be to subsidize their wages or—better yet—help them acquire the skills needed to earn more on their own.

An increase in the minimum wage to, say, $4.35 would restore the purchasing power of bottom-tier wages. It would also permit a minimum-wage breadwinner to earn almost enough to keep a family of three above the official poverty line. There are catches, however. It would increase employers' incentives to evade the law, expanding the underground economy. More important, it would increase unemployment: Raise the legal minimum price of labor above the productivity of the least skilled workers and fewer will be hired.

If a higher minimum means fewer jobs, why does it remain on the agenda of some liberals? A higher minimum would undoubtedly raise the living standard of the majority of low-wage workers who could keep their jobs. That gain, it is argued, would justify the sacrifice of the minority who became unemployable. The argument isn't convincing. Those at greatest risk from a higher minimum would be young, poor workers, who already face formidable barriers to getting and keeping jobs. Indeed, President Reagan has proposed a lower minimum wage just to improve their chances of finding work.

Perhaps the mistake here is to accept the limited terms of the debate. The working poor obviously deserve a better shake. But it should not surpass our ingenuity or generosity to help some of them without hurting others. Here are two means toward that end:

➲ Wage supplements. Government might subsidize low wages with cash or payments for medical insurance, pensions or Social Security taxes. Alternatively, Washington could enlarge the existing earned income tax credit, a "negative" income tax paying up to $800 a year to working poor families. This would permit better targeting, since minimum-wage workers in affluent families would not be eligible.

➲ Training and education. The alternative to supplementing income for the least skilled workers is to raise their earning power in a free labor market. In the last two decades, dozens of programs to do that have produced mixed results at a very high cost. But the concept isn't necessarily at fault; nurturing the potential of individuals raised in poverty is very difficult. A humane society would learn from its mistakes and keep trying.

The idea of using a minimum wage to overcome poverty is old, honorable—and fundamentally flawed. It's time to put this hoary debate behind us, and find a better way to improve the lives of people who work very hard for very little.

"Don't Raise the Minimum Wage"
(Apr. 15, 1987, p. 20)

Democratic legislators are right to search for ways to help the working poor, but wrong to think that raising the minimum wage is one of them. To do that would hurt many low-income workers, something legislators need to grasp before ramming a bill through Congress.

Senator Edward Kennedy and Representative Augustus Hawkins, Democratic chairmen of the Congressional Labor Committees, propose raising the minimum wage in three annual steps to $4.65 an hour, from $3.35, where it has stood since 1981. According to a spokesman, Senator Kennedy considers raising the minimum wage as "something like an anti-poverty program for the working poor without any Federal spending." That last part is especially seductive in a time of budget restraints.

Congress has increasingly been putting more burden on employers, like higher minimum wages or particular health and welfare benefits, as the Federal deficit has made Government financing harder. These requirements amount to a hidden tax. In the case of the minimum wage, the tax is on the jobs of those at the lowest rung. At $3.35 an hour, the minimum wage has lost 27 percent in purchasing power since 1981. A full-time worker at that rate earns less than $7,000 a year. Even at $4.65 an hour, the worker would earn less than $10,000, not even reaching the poverty level.

But the increase would come out of the hides of other working poor people. Employers are bound to circumvent a higher minimum wage in two ways: by evading the law through underground, sub-minimum hiring or by letting workers go. A higher minimum wage would probably price many working poor people out of jobs, since they could not demonstrate the productivity necessary to justify the higher wage.

Advocates argue that no one has proved that previous increases in the minimum wage cost jobs. Yet the Administration and many economists argue that a lower minimum wage is needed—to create jobs for unemployed young people. The proponents also argue that, even if some jobs are lost from a higher minimum, the overall benefit to the working poor will offset it. That's an argument likely to persuade only those whose jobs are secure.

There are at least two other approaches toward the same goal of helping the working poor, neither with the negative side effects of a higher minimum wage. In the short run, the Government could supplement the wages of working poor families. The vehicle for doing so already exists in the Earned Income Tax Credit, a kind of negative income tax.

Ultimately, the working poor would be helped most by gaining the job training and skills necessary to qualify for higher paying jobs. Senator Kennedy recognizes this, as is evident from his Jobs for Employable Dependent Individuals program for welfare recipients, recently passed by the Senate. But if there is any group that skills enhancement can help, it is the working poor, who already possess the work ethic.

The Government has not been notably successful in job and skills training in the past, but that's no reason to quit trying. Either income subsidies or training would do more for the working poor than raising the minimum wage. Such a raise may sound good; it probably does harm.

INDEX